OPPOSING
VIEWPOINTS®
SERIES

The European Union

Other Books of Related Interest:

Opposing Viewpoints Series

Democracy

Nation-Building

Current Controversies Series

Globalization

"Congress shall make no law . . . abridging the freedom of speech, or of the press."

First Amendment to the U.S. Constitution

The basic foundation of our democracy is the First Amendment guarantee of freedom of expression. The *Opposing Viewpoints* Series is dedicated to the concept of this basic freedom and the idea that it is more important to practice it than to enshrine it.

The European Union

Noël Merino, Book Editor

GREENHAVEN PRESS
A part of Gale, Cengage Learning

GALE
CENGAGE Learning

Detroit • New York • San Francisco • New Haven, Conn • Waterville, Maine • London

Christine Nasso, *Publisher*
Elizabeth Des Chenes, *Managing Editor*

© 2008 Greenhaven Press, a part of Gale, Cengage Learning

Gale and Greenhaven Press are registered trademarks used herein under license.

For more information, contact:
Greenhaven Press
27500 Drake Rd.
Farmington Hills, MI 48331-3535
Or you can visit our Internet site at gale.cengage.com

For product information and technology assistance, contact us at

Gale Customer Support, 1-800-877-4253
For permission to use material from this text or product, submit all requests online at
www.cengage.com/permissions

Further permissions questions can be emailed to permissionrequest@cengage.com

Articles in Greenhaven Press anthologies are often edited for length to meet page requirements. In addition, original titles of these works are changed to clearly present the main thesis and to explicitly indicate the author's opinion. Every effort is made to ensure that Greenhaven Press accurately reflects the original intent of the authors. Every effort has been made to trace the owners of copyrighted material.

Cover photograph © AP/Image Source.

LIBRARY OF CONGRESS CATALOGING-IN-PUBLICATION DATA

The European Union / Noël Merino, book editor.
  p. cm. -- (Opposing viewpoints)
  Includes bibliographical references and index.
  ISBN-13: 978-0-7377-3998-5 (hardcover)
  ISBN-13: 978-0-7377-3999-2 (pbk.)
  1. European Union. I. Merino, Noël.
  JN30.E94116 2009
  341.242'2--dc22

                                                                    2008008893

Printed in the United States of America
2 3 4 5 6   26 25 24 23 22

Contents

Why Consider Opposing Viewpoints?   11

Introduction   14

Chapter 1: What Do European Union Member States Want for Their Future?

Chapter Preface   19

1. European Union Members Are Divided in   21
   Their Vision of the Future
   Jeffrey Kopstein

2. The European Union's Future Should Be   26
   Defined by the Pursuit of Six Shared Goals
   Timothy Garton Ash

3. Disagreement over the European Union   37
   Constitution Is a Hopeful Sign for Democracy
   Gary Younge

4. Nationalism Will Always Be More Powerful   42
   than Allegiance to the European Union
   Patrick J. Buchanan

5. The European Union Needs to Become   47
   More Centralized and Define Its Future
   Charles Kupchan

Periodical Bibliography   53

Chapter 2: What Countries Should Be Members of the European Union?

Chapter Preface   55

1. The European Union Will Continue to Expand   57
   Hans-Juergen Zahorka

2. The European Union Faces Hurdles to   67
   Continued Expansion
   The Economist

3. Turkey Should Be Allowed to Join the
   European Union
   Orhan Pamuk   72

4. Turkey Should Not Be Allowed to Join the
   European Union
   Tom Spencer   77

5. Great Britain Should Leave the European Union   83
   Vernon Coleman

6. Great Britain Should Remain in the
   European Union
   Richard Laming   89

Periodical Bibliography   95

Chapter 3: Is the European Union Succeeding Globally?

Chapter Preface   97

1. America Can Maintain Global Security on
   Its Own
   Robert Kagan   99

2. America Needs the Help of the European
   Union for Global Security
   Ronald D. Asmus and Kenneth M. Pollack   106

3. The Economy of the European Union Is Not
   Doing Well
   Richard W. Rahn   114

4. The Economy of the European Union Is
   Doing Well
   Olivier J. Blanchard   119

5. Europe's Employment Practices Hurt the
   European Union Economy
   Bruce Bartlett   124

6. Europe's Employment Practices Do Not Hurt   129
the European Union Economy
Thomas Geoghegan

7. Airbus and Other European Companies Get   135
Unfair Advantages
Investor's Business Daily

8. Airbus and Other European Companies   140
Are Thriving Fair and Square
Floyd J. McKay

Periodical Bibliography   145

Chapter 4: What Should the EU Do About Its Diverse Nationalities and Languages?

Chapter Preface   147

1. A European Identity Is Compatible with   149
National Identity
Kyle James

2. There Is No European Identity, Only   155
National Identity
Daniel Hannan

3. The European Union's Many Official   160
Languages Create Challenges
James Owen

4. The European Union's Many Official   166
Languages Are Necessary
European Commission

5. French Should Be the Official Language of   172
the European Union
Dan Bilefsky

Periodical Bibliography   177
For Further Discussion   178

Organizations to Contact   181
Bibliography of Books   186
Index   189

Why Consider Opposing Viewpoints?

"The only way in which a human being can make some approach to knowing the whole of a subject is by hearing what can be said about it by persons of every variety of opinion and studying all modes in which it can be looked at by every character of mind. No wise man ever acquired his wisdom in any mode but this."

John Stuart Mill

In our media-intensive culture it is not difficult to find differing opinions. Thousands of newspapers and magazines and dozens of radio and television talk shows resound with differing points of view. The difficulty lies in deciding which opinion to agree with and which "experts" seem the most credible. The more inundated we become with differing opinions and claims, the more essential it is to hone critical reading and thinking skills to evaluate these ideas. *Opposing Viewpoints* books address this problem directly by presenting stimulating debates that can be used to enhance and teach these skills. The varied opinions contained in each book examine many different aspects of a single issue. While examining these conveniently edited opposing views, readers can develop critical thinking skills such as the ability to compare and contrast authors' credibility, facts, argumentation styles, use of persuasive techniques, and other stylistic tools. In short, the *Opposing Viewpoints* Series is an ideal way to attain the higher-level thinking and reading skills so essential in a culture of diverse and contradictory opinions.

In addition to providing a tool for critical thinking, *Opposing Viewpoints* books challenge readers to question their own strongly held opinions and assumptions. Most people form their opinions on the basis of upbringing, peer pressure, and personal, cultural, or professional bias. By reading carefully balanced opposing views, readers must directly confront new ideas as well the opinions of those with whom they disagree. This is not to simplistically argue that everyone who reads opposing views will—or should—change his or her opinion. Instead, the series enhances readers' understanding of their own views by encouraging confrontation with opposing ideas. Careful examination of others' views can lead to the readers' understanding of the logical inconsistencies in their own opinions, perspective on why they hold an opinion, and the consideration of the possibility that their opinion requires further evaluation.

Evaluating Other Opinions

To ensure that this type of examination occurs, *Opposing Viewpoints* books present all types of opinions. Prominent spokespeople on different sides of each issue as well as well-known professionals from many disciplines challenge the reader. An additional goal of the series is to provide a forum for other, less known, or even unpopular viewpoints. The opinion of an ordinary person who has had to make the decision to cut off life support from a terminally ill relative, for example, may be just as valuable and provide just as much insight as a medical ethicist's professional opinion. The editors have two additional purposes in including these less known views. One, the editors encourage readers to respect others' opinions—even when not enhanced by professional credibility. It is only by reading or listening to and objectively evaluating others' ideas that one can determine whether they are worthy of consideration. Two, the inclusion of such viewpoints encourages the important critical thinking skill of objectively evaluating an author's credentials and bias. This evaluation will illuminate an author's reasons for taking a particular stance on an issue and will aid in readers' evaluation of the author's ideas.

It is our hope that these books will give readers a deeper understanding of the issues debated and an appreciation of the complexity of even seemingly simple issues when good and honest people disagree. This awareness is particularly important in a democratic society such as ours in which people enter into public debate to determine the common good. Those with whom one disagrees should not be regarded as enemies but rather as people whose views deserve careful examination and may shed light on one's own.

Thomas Jefferson once said that "difference of opinion leads to inquiry, and inquiry to truth." Jefferson, a broadly educated man, argued that "if a nation expects to be ignorant and free . . . it expects what never was and never will be." As individuals and as a nation, it is imperative that we consider the opinions of others and examine them with skill and discernment. The *Opposing Viewpoints* Series is intended to help readers achieve this goal.

David L. Bender and Bruno Leone,
Founders

Introduction

"The economic contribution of visitors and migrants is nothing new. At crucial points over the past century and beyond we have relied on migrants to supply essential capital to our economy and plug the labor gaps when no others could be found." —Tony Blair, Speech to the Confederation of British Industry, April 27, 2004.

As of 2007, the European Union (EU) includes twenty-seven member countries. As the European Union has grown, the issue of immigration has become an especially challenging one. The appropriate policy toward fellow EU citizens among EU member states is hotly contested, especially since the admission of ten Eastern European countries to the union.

The origin of the European Union can be traced to the Treaty of Rome in 1957 among the countries of Belgium, France, Italy, Luxembourg, the Netherlands, and West Germany. This treaty established the European Economic Community (EEC) and has since become known as the Treaty Establishing the European Community (TEC). Denmark, Ireland, and the United Kingdom (UK)—comprising England, Northern Ireland, Scotland, and Wales—joined in 1973, while the 1980s saw the addition of Greece, Portugal, and Spain. The 1990s added East Germany as part of German reunification, as well as adding the countries of Austria, Finland, and Sweden. At the beginning of the millennium, the European Union was comprised of those fifteen countries.

In 2004 the European Union had its most dramatic enlargement, with the addition of ten countries: Cyprus, the

Czech Republic, Estonia, Hungary, Latvia, Lithuania, Malta, Poland, Slovakia, and Slovenia. Less than three years later, in 2007, Bulgaria and Romania joined. The twenty-first-century enlargement, with most of the countries from Eastern Europe, has heated up the discussion about immigration among member states.

In 1985, the Schengen Agreement abolished many of the border controls between the countries of the European Union, allowing for common policies toward visitors and police co-operation across borders. With a few exceptions, the agreement also allows for movement without visas throughout the European Union for citizens of member states. But concerning the ability to live and work permanently, or to immigrate, the situation is not quite as simple.

With the Maastricht Treaty of 1992 came the name "European Union" and the concept of EU citizenship, allowing each European citizen the right to move and reside freely throughout the European Union, without reference to an economic activity. While the fifteen countries of the twentieth-century European Union, Cyprus, and Malta enjoy this freedom, the ten newest member countries from Eastern Europe did not get immediate full membership to this agreement regarding the free movement of workers (EU countries can restrict workers until 2011). Individual EU member countries have their own policies; some countries, like the United Kingdom and Ireland, have allowed the newest EU citizens to apply for worker residency permits and have accepted many new immigrants. Other countries, fearing a mass influx of laborers willing to work for modest wages, put restrictions on the newest Eastern European members at the time of accession.

The United Kingdom allowed citizens of the eight admitted Eastern Europe countries of 2004 free access to its labor markets, while restricting access to Bulgarians and Romanians. In May 2007, BBC News reported, "640,000 workers from Eastern Europe have sought work in the UK since the EU expanded in May 2004." Among those applications, approximately 613,000 were approved to work in the United Kingdom. The Home Office of the United Kingdom reports that the country with the largest number of immigrant workers during the three-year period, by far, is Poland, with almost 400,000 approved workers.

Among countries that have allowed Eastern European workers, the reviews have been mixed. While Polish immigrant workers have poured into Britain and Ireland, a March 26, 2007, *Time* magazine article reports that "rather than undermine local economies, their enterprise and skills have helped the British and Irish economies remain robust. Conversely, unemployment is higher in France, which turned Poles away." Many have argued that immigrant workers in the United Kingdom take jobs that no one else wants, but some claim that the immigrants are having a negative impact on wages. Sir Andrew Green, Chairman of Migration Watch UK, argues that British workers are being replaced by Eastern European workers who will work for less: "If anyone accepts a low enough wage, they are likely to get a job." In fact, Green argues that "95% of the first wave of East Europeans are earning less than £8 an hour [minimum wage is £5.3 an hour]." Larry Miller, CBS News correspondent in London says, "Yes, new immigrants tend to undercut British labor prices, but most people buy on quality. It just so happens that the Polish workers I'm using are more expensive, and they are worth every cent." Miller believes that the new immigrant workers are doing so well because they possess a strong work ethic and skills, something he sees lacking in native Britons.

Whether the member states of the European Union will be able to abide by the free movement of workers agreement in the coming years remains to be seen. It depends on the economic health of the Eastern European countries, the economies of the rest of Europe, public opinion on immigration, and levels of nationalism. This debate is just one among many contentious issues surrounding the developing European Union.

The authors of *Opposing Viewpoints: The European Union* debate current issues regarding the European Union in the following chapters: What Do European Union Member States Want for Their Future? What Countries Should Be Members of the European Union? Is the European Union Succeeding Globally? and What Should the EU Do About Its Diverse Nationalities and Languages? The many viewpoints included in this volume reflect the wide disagreement about the future of the European Union, which will continue to offer much opportunity for debate.

OPPOSING VIEWPOINTS® SERIES

CHAPTER 1

What Do European Union Member States Want for Their Future?

Chapter Preface

The Public Opinion Analysis sector of the European Commission monitors the evolution of public opinion in the member states of the European Union (EU) on major topics such as enlargement, health, culture, defense, and the environment. *Eurobarometer* surveys were performed in November and December 2006 of over twenty-five thousand Europeans from the twenty-seven EU countries, including Bulgaria and Romania, which joined in January 2007. The results reported in February 2007 show a general picture of Europeans' view of their current situation, their concerns, and their trust in politics.

European Union citizens, when asked to compare their current personal situation to the situation of five years ago, largely believed it had improved: 39 percent said it improved, 35 percent said it had not changed, and 25 percent said it had deteriorated. The younger the citizen, the more likely they were to think things had improved, with 59 percent of people aged fifteen to twenty-four saying that their personal situation had improved. As far as looking into the future, 41 percent believed that their situation would improve over the next five years.

When asked about their issues of concern, unemployment was at the top of the list, with 36 percent voicing concern about this issue. Nonetheless, approximately 85 percent of the European workforce polled stated that they were confident in their ability to keep their job in the coming months. The second two most commonly voiced concerns were the cost of living (30 percent) together with concern about pensions (30 percent), followed by crime (26 percent), health care (26 percent), and terrorism (25 percent). Only 14 percent voiced concern about immigration and only 8 percent worried about the integration of foreigners. On the question of immigration,

48 percent believed that immigrants were needed to do certain work, but 46 percent thought that the presence of people from other ethnic groups increased unemployment in their country.

When it comes to politics, Europeans are not enthusiastic. Only 43 percent thought politics is important and the vast majority have little trust for their political institutions: Less than one-third of EU citizens trust their country's national political system (government and parliament). While the survey did not explicitly ask members about their trust in the European Commission, since respondents indicated that they had less trust for political bodies as they became more distant (trusting local political entities the most) one can only guess that the view would not be favorable.

The surveys performed by the European Commission show that Europeans have widely differing views about how they are doing and what concerns they have. These views are debated by the authors in the following chapter.

> *"The middle-aged EU is facing new and daunting challenges, some of which do not appear to have easy solutions."*

European Union Members Are Divided in Their Vision of the Future

Jeffrey Kopstein

In the following viewpoint, Jeffrey Kopstein claims that members of the European Union (EU) are deeply divided about what the future should look like. He argues that the EU member states need to come to some agreement on a vision of the future. Kopstein identifies legitimacy, enlargement, and defense as some of the most pressing challenges facing the EU. Jeffrey Kopstein is director of the Institute of European Studies at the Munk Centre for International Studies in Toronto and professor of political science at the University of Toronto.

As you read, consider the following questions:

1. What does Kopstein identify as two of the European Union's biggest successes?

Jeffrey Kopstein, "Europe: Who and How?" *Globe and Mail*, March 23, 2007. www .theglobeandmail.com. Reproduced by permission.

2. According to the author, what are two different answers to the question, "What is the EU?"

3. What does Kopstein claim is the European Union's most serious problem?

This month [March 2007] marks the 50th anniversary of the European Union's [EU's] founding agreement, the Treaty of Rome, but Europeans remain deeply divided about what the union is, who should be let in and what Europe's global role should be. How they resolve these disputes will determine the continent's fate for the next half-century.

The EU's First Fifty Years

It is important to recall that the Treaty of Rome was preceded by an earlier attempt at a coal and steel union, which tells us a great deal about its purpose. After the Second World War, the political leadership of France, Germany, and the other countries of Europe understood that any durable peace required pooling their ability to manufacture the implements of war.

Yet, partial integration was not enough. Integration in one area quickly spilled over into others. This powerful logic pushed Germany, France, the rest of Europe toward much deeper economic and political co-operation—a logic, incidentally, that is now just as much at work in North America as in Europe.

The end result is impressive by any standard. A European bloc with a single currency that is rich and at peace. Young people now travel effortlessly from Spain to Slovenia without ever noticing a border, and senior citizens from England retire in France or Portugal, receiving their pension cheques by local post and health care from local doctors without thinking twice.

Beyond peace between Germany and France, Europe's biggest success may be in taking poor or authoritarian states and helping them become rich democracies. Ireland, which joined

Europe in 1973 as an economic basket case, is now known as the Celtic tiger. Spain and Portugal, which entered in 1986 as wobbly post-fascist democracies with Third World economies, are now the California and Oregon of Europe. And who would have thought Belgian and German economists would envy Poland and Estonia for their economic flexibility?

Challenges for the EU's Future

Even with these successes, the middle-aged EU is facing new and daunting challenges, some of which do not appear to have easy solutions. First is the question of legitimacy. From the outset, European integration has been an elite-driven project, negotiated by diplomats in treaty language impenetrable even to trained lawyers. As long as the union didn't appear to affect the lives of ordinary Europeans, nobody cared. But regulations pouring out of Brussels [Belgium, site of the EU executive branch headquarters] now includes everything from domestic security to the transportation of geese.

Both member states and citizens have begun to push back, asking, "What is the EU?" Some Europeans see it primarily [as] a free-trade zone of sovereign states. Others consider it a new kind of federal state. Brussels bureaucrats carefully tiptoe around this question, but the failure of the European Constitution in referendums in France and the Netherlands in 2005 signalled that the gap between European institutions and the citizenry is now dangerously large. [Leading] European philosopher Juergen Habermas called for the creation of a directly elected EU president and foreign minister, a good idea that will probably go nowhere.

The public-opinion gap is especially large on the question of further enlargement. Bulgaria and Romania barely made it in at the beginning of this year [2007], with Europe's leaders increasingly feeling that the union has grown too large and too fast. Although negotiations formally continue on Turkey,

EU Member Countries, 2008

actual admission will require a sea change in public opinion, especially in a country such as France, where a referendum will be held on the matter.

Europe's political elites have refused to do the necessary spade work of preparing public opinion for Turkish membership. Instead, they remain inward looking, uncomfortable with multiculturalism, always worried about the next domestic election. In doing so, they fail to consider the broader implications of refusing Turkey altogether. If left out, Turkey will pursue its own security agenda, and in the context of a nuclearizing Iran, that can only mean developing its own nuclear program. Who could blame them?

In fact, the inability to engage in geopolitics is probably the EU's most serious problem. Defending the union's most basic interests will one day require warfare, and that is something the bloc refuses to consider. The EU's basic security documents do not even discuss the use of force. Instead they require any military operation to win the approval of the United Nations Security Council, effectively giving China a veto over EU foreign policy. As long as the EU possesses neither the ability nor the collective will to use hard power, it will not be taken as seriously as it desires on the international stage.

Fifty years after its "founding," Europe needs to re-engage. But thinking geopolitically will require some sort of compelling vision that exceeds the union's original vision. Europe's mandate is no longer just about peace. Ironically, what the continent looks like 50 years from now will depend upon the power of the European imagination to think beyond its own borders.

"We don't know why we have an EU or what it's good for. So we urgently need a new narrative."

The European Union's Future Should Be Defined by the Pursuit of Six Shared Goals

Timothy Garton Ash

In the following viewpoint, Timothy Garton Ash argues that the European Union (EU) needs to develop a united vision of the future. Ash proposes that this new vision be guided by six shared European goals: freedom, peace, law, prosperity, diversity, and solidarity. Ash explains each of the six proposed goals and discusses current shortcomings related to each. Timothy Garton Ash is a professor of European studies at Oxford University and the author of Free World.

As you read, consider the following questions:

1. According to the author, what are the current shortcomings of European Union member states' political processes that threaten the goal of freedom?

2. What is the relationship between EU law and the national law of member states, according to Ash?

3. What does the author cite as a success of the European Union's commitment to solidarity among countries in the EU?

Most Europeans now have little idea where we're coming from; far less do we share a vision of where we want to go to. We don't know why we have an EU [European Union] or what it's good for. So we urgently need a new narrative.

I propose that our new story should be woven from six strands, each of which represents a shared European goal. The strands are freedom, peace, law, prosperity, diversity and solidarity. None of these goals is unique to Europe, but most Europeans would agree that it is characteristic of contemporary Europe to aspire to them. Our performance, however, often falls a long way short of the aspiration. That falling short is itself part of our new story and must be spelled out. For today's Europe should also have a capacity for constant self-criticism. . . .

Freedom

Europe's history over the last 65 years is a story of the spread of freedom. In 1942, there were only four perilously free countries in Europe: Britain, Switzerland, Sweden, Ireland. By 1962 most of western Europe was free, except for Spain and Portugal. In 1982 the Iberian peninsula [Spain and Portugal] had joined the free, as had Greece, but most of what we then called eastern Europe was under communist dictatorship. Today, among countries that may definitely be accounted European, there is only one nasty little authoritarian regime left—Belarus. Most Europeans now live in liberal democracies. That has never before been the case; not in 2,500 years. And it's worth celebrating.

A majority of the EU's current member states were dictatorships within living memory. Italy's president, Giorgio Napolitano, has a vivid recollection of [Benito] Mussolini's fascist regime. The president of the European commission, José Manuel Barroso, grew up under [Antonio de Olveira] Salazar's dictatorship in Portugal. The EU's foreign policy chief, Javier Solana, remembers dodging General [Francisco] Franco's police. Eleven of the 27 heads of government who will gather round the table at the spring European council, including the German chancellor Angela Merkel, were subjects of communist dictatorships less than 20 years ago. They know what freedom is because they know what unfreedom is.

To be sure, people living under dictatorships wanted to be free mainly because they wanted to be free, not because they wanted to be EU-ropean. But the prospect of joining what is now the EU has encouraged country after country, from Spain and Portugal 30 years ago to Croatia and Turkey today, to transform its domestic politics, economy, law, media and society. The EU is one of the most successful engines of peaceful regime change ever. For decades, the struggle for freedom and what is emotively called the "return to Europe" have gone arm in arm.

Shortcomings: Closer examination shows that many of Europe's newer democracies are seriously flawed, with high levels of corruption—especially, but by no means only, in southeastern Europe. Money also speaks too loudly in the politics, legal systems and media of our established democracies, as it does in the US. Whatever the theory, in practice rich Europeans are more free than poor ones. The EU is a great catalyst of democracy but it is not itself very democratic. EU regulations are justified in the name of the treaty of Rome's "four freedoms," the free movement of goods, people, services and capital—but these regulations can themselves be infringements of individual freedom. Anyway, the EU can't claim all the credt: the US, Nato [North Atlantic Treaty Organization] and the Organisation for Security and Co-operation in Europe have also played a major part in securing Europeans' freedoms. Until recently, the defence of individual human rights and civil liberties has been more the province of the Council of Europe and its European court of human rights than of the EU.

Peace

For centuries, Europe was a theatre of war. Now it is a theatre of peace. Instead of trying out our national strengths on the battlefield, we do it on the football field. Disputes between European nations are resolved in endless negotiations in Brussels [Belgium, site of the EU executive branch headquarters], not by armed conflict. The EU is a system of permanent, institutionalised conflict resolution. If you get tired of Brussels waffle and fudge, contemplate the alternative. It may seem to you unthinkable that French and Germans would ever fight each other again, but Serbs and Albanians were killing each other only the day before yesterday. You cannot simply rely on goodwill to keep the peace in Europe. This may be an old, familiar argument for European integration but that does not make it less true. Sometimes the old arguments are still the best.

Shortcomings: We cannot prove it was European integration that kept the peace in western Europe after 1945. Others would claim it was Nato and the hegemonic system of the cold war, with the US functioning as "Europe's pacifier"; others again would cite the fact that western Europe became a zone of liberal democracies, and liberal democracies don't go to war with each other. Several things happened at once and historians can argue about their relative weight. Anyway, central and eastern Europe did not live at peace after 1945: witness the Soviet tanks rolling into East Berlin [East Germany], Budapest [Hungary] and Prague [Czechoslovakia], and the "state of war" declared in Poland in 1981. Moreover, Europe—in the sense of the EU and, more broadly, the established democracies of Europe—failed to prevent war returning to the continent after the end of the cold war. Twice it took US intervention to stop war in the Balkans. So what are we so proud of?

Law

Most Europeans, most of the time, live under the rule of law. We enjoy codified human and civil rights and we can go to court to protect those rights. If we don't receive satisfaction in local and national courts, we have recourse to European ones—including the European court of human rights. Men and women, rich and poor, black and white, heterosexual and homosexual, are equal before the law. By and large, we can assume that the police are there to defend us, rather than advancing the interests of those in power, doing the bidding of the local mafia or lining their own pockets. We forget how unusual this is. For most of European history, most Europeans did not live under the rule of law. At least two thirds of humankind still does not today. "I have a gun, so I decide what the law is," an African officer at a roadblock told a journalist of my acquaintance, before pocketing an arbitrary "fine."

The EU is a community of law. The treaty of Rome, and succeeding treaties, have been turned into a kind of constitution by the work of European courts. One scholar has described the European court of justice as "the most effective supranational judicial body in the history of the world." EU law takes priority over national law. Even the strongest governments and corporations must eventually yield to the rulings of European judges. Why are the leading European football teams full of players from other countries? Because of a 1995 ruling of the court of Justice. It is thanks to the judicial enforcement of European laws on the "four freedoms" that most Europeans can now travel, shop, live and work wherever they like in most of Europe.

Shortcomings: In practice, some are more equal than others. Look at [former Italian prime minister] Silvio Berlusconi.

The Growth of a European Identity

Defining 'Europe' and 'European' has always been difficult, thanks to disagreements about the outer limits of the region and the inner character of its inhabitants. Today those inhabitants are experiencing political and economic change that is encouraging them to think of themselves less as Spaniards or Belgians or Poles and more as 'Europeans', but this is a trend that begs several questions. What is Europe, where does it begin and end, and what exactly does being a European mean? Is there a coherent and distinctive European identity and a set of core European values with which the inhabitants of the region can identify? When and how did the idea of European unity emerge, and how has it evolved?

Europe has never been united, and its history has been one of fragmentation, conflict, and changing political boundaries. Large parts of Europe have been brought together at various times for different reasons—beginning with the Romans and moving through the Franks to the Habsburgs, Napoleon, and [Adolf] Hitler—but while many have dreamed of unification, it has only been since the Second World War that Europeans have finally begun to embrace the notion that nationalism might be put aside in the interests of regional cooperation. For the first time in its history, almost the entire region is engaged in a process of integration that is encouraging its inhabitants to think and behave as Europeans rather than as members of smaller cultural or national groups that just happen to inhabit the same land mass.

John McCormick,
Understanding the European Union, *2005.*

And there are still large areas of lawlessness, especially in eastern and southeastern Europe. In established democracies, security powers, including detention without trial, have been stepped up, violating civil liberties in the name of the "war on terror." And the primacy of European law and the power of judges is, of course, precisely what Eurosceptics—especially in Britain—hate. They see it as stripping power from the democratically elected parliaments of sovereign states.

Prosperity

Most Europeans are better off than their parents, and much better off than their grandparents. They live in more comfortable, warmer, safer accommodation; eat richer, more varied food; have larger disposable incomes; enjoy more interesting holidays. We have never had it so good. Look at Henri Cartier-Bresson's wonderful book of photographs, Europeans, and you will be reminded just how poor many Europeans still were in the 1950s. If you represent the countries of the world on a map according to the size of their gross domestic product [GDP], and shade them according to GDP per head, you can see that Europe is one of the richest blocks in the world.

Shortcomings: Bond Street [high-end shopping district in London] and the Kurfürstendamm [high-end shopping district in Berlin] are not typical of Europe. There are still pockets of shaming poverty, even in Europe's richest countries, and there are some very poor countries in Europe's east. It is also very hard to establish how much of this prosperity is due to the existence of the EU. In his book *Europe Reborn*, the economic historian Harold James reproduces a graph that shows how GDP per capita in France, Germany and Britain grew throughout the 20th century, with large dips in the two world wars from which we recovered with rapid postwar growth. Overall, prosperity grew at roughly the same rate in the first half of the century, when we didn't have the European Economic Community, as in the second half, when we did. The main reason for this steady growth, James suggests, is the development and application of technology. The EU's single market and competition policy have almost certainly enhanced our prosperity; policies like the CAP [Common Agricultural Policy], and extra costs incurred due to EU regulations and social policy, have almost certainly not. Countries like Switzerland and Norway have done well outside the EU. In any case, the glory days of European growth are far behind us. In the last decade, the more advanced European economies have grown more slowly than the US, and far more slowly than the emerging giants of Asia.

Diversity

In an essay entitled "Among the Euroweenies," the American humorist PJ O'Rourke once complained about Europe's proliferation of "dopey little countries." "Even the languages are itty-bitty," he groaned. "Sometimes you need two or three just to get you through till lunch." But that's just what I love about Europe. You can enjoy one culture, cityscape, media and cuisine in the morning, and then, with a short hop by plane or train, enjoy another that same evening. And yet another the next day. And when I say "you," I don't just mean a tiny elite. Students travelling with easyJet [a discount airline] and Polish plumbers [a euphemism for low-paid, Eastern European immigrant laborers] on overnight coaches can appreciate it too.

Europe is an intricate, multicoloured patchwork. Every national (and sub-national) culture has its own specialities and beauties. Each itty-bitty language reveals a subtly different way of life and thought, ripened over centuries. The British say, "What on earth does that mean?"; the Germans, "What in heaven should that mean?" (was im Himmel soll das bedeuten?): philosophical empiricism and idealism captured in one everyday phrase. Awantura in Polish means a big, loud, yet secretly rather enjoyable quarrel. Bella figura in Italian is an untranslatable notion of how a man or woman should wish to be in the company of other men and women.

This is not just diversity; it is peaceful, managed and nurtured diversity. America has riches and Africa has variety, but only Europe combines such riches and such variety in so compact a space.

Shortcomings: This is the strand on which I can see the least credible criticism, Eurosceptics decry the EU as a homogenising force, driving out old-fashioned national specialities like handmade Italian cheese (with delicious added handgrime) or British beef and beer measured in imperial pounds and pints. But the examples are not so numerous, and for every element of old-fashioned diversity closed down by EU regulation there are two new ones opened up, from the Caffè Nero on a British high street to the cheap weekend trip to Prague. Europeanisation is generally a less homogenising version of globalisation than is Americanisation.

Solidarity

Isn't this the most characteristic value of today's Europe? We believe that economic growth should be seasoned with social justice, free enterprise balanced by social security—and we have European laws and national welfare states to make it so. Europe's social democrats and Christian democrats agree that a market economy should not mean a market society. There must be no American-style, social Darwinian capitalist jungle here, with the poor and weak left to die in the gutter.

We also believe in solidarity between richer and poorer countries and regions inside the EU, hence the EU funds from which countries like Ireland and Portugal have benefited so visibly over the last two decades. And we believe in solidarity between the world's rich north and its poor south—hence our generous national and EU aid budgets and our commitment to slow down global warming, which will disproportionately hurt some of the world's poorest.

Shortcomings: This is the strand where Europe's reality falls painfully short of its aspiration, there is a significant solidarity, mediated by the state, in the richer European countries, but even in our most prosperous cities we still have beggars and homeless people sleeping rough. In the poorer countries of eastern Europe, the welfare state exists mainly on paper. To be poor, old and sick in Europe's wild east is no more pleasant than it is to be poor, old and sick in America's wild west. Yes, there were big financial transfers to countries like Portugal, Ireland and Greece, but those to the new member states of the EU today are much meaner. In the period 2004–06, the "old" 15 member states contributed an average of £26 per citizen per year into the EU budget for enlargement—so our trans-European solidarity amounted to the price of a cup of coffee each month. As for solidarity with the rest of the world, the EU comes top of Oxfam's "double standards index," measuring protectionist practices in the rich north. Our agricultural protectionism is as bad as anyone's, and the EU is responsible, with the US, for the shameful stalling of the Doha round of world trade talks [which began in 2001].

EU as Family Likeness

These are, I repeat, merely notes towards a new European story. Perhaps we need to add or subtract a theme or two. The flesh then has to be put on the bare bones. Popular attachment, let alone enthusiasm, will not be generated by a list of six abstract nouns. Everything depends on the personalities, events and anecdotes that give life and colour to narrative. These will vary from place to place. The stories of European freedom, peace or diversity can and should be told differently in Warsaw [Poland] and Madrid [Spain], on the left and on the right. There need be no single one-size-fits-all version of our story—no narrative equivalent of the eurozone interest rate. Indeed to impose uniformity in the praise of diversity would be a contradiction. Nonetheless, given the same bone structure, the fleshed-out stories told in Finnish, Italian, Swedish or French will have a strong family likeness, just as European cities do.

Woven together, the six strands will add up to an account of where we have come from and a vision of where we want to go. Different strands will, however, appeal more strongly to different people. For me, the most inspiring stories are those of freedom and diversity. I acknowledge the others with my head but those are the two that quicken my heart. They are the reason I can say, without hyperbole, that I love Europe. Not in the same sense that I love my family, of course; nothing compares with that. Not even in the sense that I love England, although on a rainy day it runs it close. But there is a meaningful sense in which I can say that I love Europe—in other words, that I am a European patriot.

Our new European story will never generate the kind of fiery allegiances that were characteristic of the pre-1914 nation state. Today's Europe is not like that—fortunately. Our enterprise does not need or even want that kind of emotional fire. Europeanness remains a secondary, cooler identity. Europeans today are not called upon to die for Europe. Most of us are not even called upon to live for Europe. All that is required is that we should let Europe live.

"The only thing more staggering than the pace of European integration over the past fifteen years has been the lack of accountability that has gone with it."

Disagreement over the European Union Constitution Is a Hopeful Sign for Democracy

Gary Younge

In the following viewpoint, Gary Younge argues that the failure of the European Union (EU) Constitution shows how out of touch EU leadership is from the citizens of EU member states. Younge claims that the rejection of the constitution by France and the Netherlands is a positive step toward making the European Union more democratic. Younge is the Alfred Knobler Journalism Fellow at the Nation Institute and the New York correspondent for The Guardian.

As you read, consider the following questions:

1. According to the author, what were some of the components of the European Union Constitution?

Gary Younge, "A Win for EU Democracy," *The Nation*, June 20, 2005. www.thenation .com. Copyright © 2005 by *The Nation* Magazine/The Nation Company, Inc. Reproduced by permission.

2. Why does Younge think the French and Dutch rejection of the constitution is a positive development?

3. According to Younge, what were the two principal forces behind the no vote in France and the Netherlands?

The French said non, the Dutch said nee, and despite eighteen other official languages to choose from the Eurocrats were rendered temporarily speechless. The rejection of the European Constitution in late May and early June [2005] referendums in France and the Netherlands was the most predictable shock in the history of European integration.

The polls had long forewarned the results. Yet to imagine that two of the European Union's [EU's] founding members and most loyal devotees would take a torch to the house they themselves had built was more than the Europhiles could bear. There was no plan B.

The Rejected Constitution

The Constitution aimed to streamline and cohere all previous EU treaties following the accession of ten new members in 2004 so that the EU could operate more efficiently and talk to the rest of the world with one consistent voice. It would have completed the transition, at a breakneck speed of just over a decade, from a free-trade area of twelve nations similar to the North American Free Trade Agreement [NAFTA] to a multinational body of twenty-five countries where millions would share a court of human rights, the same-color passports, an official flag, an official currency and an official anthem ([Ludwig van] Beethoven's "Ode to Joy").

But it had to be ratified by all member states. By May 29 [2005] nine had already done so, although only Spain had taken it to the people in a referendum. With the French and Dutch rejections, it has been temporarily put on ice, its future now uncertain. Along with it in the deep freeze goes the hope of some on the left that the EU might emerge as a

more progressive geopolitical bloc that could check or challenge America's global hegemony.

For this setback, however, we should all be thankful. While the aim of pooling the resources of relatively small European nations to challenge more effectively the excesses of US supremacy, including war and rigged markets, is laudable, the undemocratic means by which the EU has chosen to go about it are lamentable.

Lack of Democracy in the EU

The only thing more staggering than the pace of European integration over the past fifteen years has been the lack of accountability that has gone with it. Neither the president of the

European Commission nor any of the commissioners, who wield most power in the EU, are elected. They are selected in rounds of horse trading by national governments on the basis of political patronage. Indeed, the European Parliament, the only directly elected component of the EU, cannot even initiate legislation. This explains why turnout for EU elections is even lower than for US presidential elections—45.5 percent last year.

There are some good things in the Constitution, which would guarantee shelter, education, collective bargaining for labor and fair working conditions. But a somewhat progressive agenda that has been imposed has less credibility than a reactionary one that has been chosen. The lack of democracy leads ineluctably to a lack of legitimacy. Unable to influence the pace, scale or direction of integration, many Europeans have become alienated from it.

Their despondency, while clearly widespread, found little or no expression in the mainstream electoral politics of either country. In the Netherlands 85 percent of parliamentarians were in favor of a yes vote, along with the employers associations, unions and almost all the newspapers. In France the establishment was similarly aligned. So the victory for the no campaigns reveals a profound dislocation between the political class and the political culture. The margins, in effect, became the mainstream. This posed challenges and opportunities for the left in both countries.

The two principal forces mobilizing the no vote were the far right (including fascists and other assorted nationalists) and the hard left (including Trotskyists, Communists, environmentalists and antiglobalization protesters). The former, which dominated the campaign in the Netherlands, circled the wagons around an ossified and xenophobic sense of nationhood, exploiting fears of open borders, Turkish accession and the threat to national identity. The latter, which had most traction in France, slammed the EU's free-market foundations, which will allow machines to chase the cheapest labor around the continent. The left did not shut the door on the Constitution altogether but argued for a body that would be more relevant, responsive, democratic and worker-friendly with the slogan, "A Different Europe Is Possible."

It is precisely with this agenda that the European left should now enter negotiations on the current, uncertain future of European integration. Beyond a slide in the euro and the meltdown in both countries, the effects will be long term. The European Constitution is dead, but the European project will continue.

A Future for Democracy

The desire to forge a more progressive counterbalance to a unipolar world with the United States at the helm is a sound one. But it won't be progressive unless it is built with the consent of those in whose name it has been created. The problem with American power is not that it is American but that, both at home and abroad, it backs the powerful against the weak and supports democracy only when democracy supports America. If Europe wants to confront that it must offer more democracy, not less. By saying no, the French and Dutch certainly slowed the European juggernaut. That was the first crucial step in putting it back on the right track.

| "Nationalism is tearing at the aging fabric of European unity."

Nationalism Will Always Be More Powerful than Allegiance to the European Union

Patrick J. Buchanan

In the following viewpoint, Patrick J. Buchanan argues that the European Union's (EU's) future is in trouble because the European Union is not a nation. The EU cannot compete, he argues, with the nationalistic feelings citizens have for their respective countries. Pointing to the lack of accomplishment of the EU, public opinion about the EU, and concerns about immigration, Buchanan believes that the EU cannot inspire the allegiance it needs to be successful. Buchanan is an author, columnist, broadcaster, and politician. He has run for U.S. president three times and is a founder of the magazine The American Conservative.

As you read, consider the following questions:

1. According to Buchanan, what do EU champions claim as the union's greatest achievement?

Patrick J. Buchanan, "The Mid-Life Crisis of the EU," *WorldNetDaily*, March 30, 2007. www.worldnetdaily.com. Reproduced by permission.

2. Do a majority of EU citizens think positively of the EU, according to the *Washington Times* poll that the author cites?

3. According to the author, what do EU citizens think about immigration?

The 50th birthday of the European Union [EU], born in Rome in March 1957 as the European Economic Community or Common Market—of Germany, France, Italy, Belgium, Holland and Luxembourg—was a pallid affair.

Understandably so. For though the EU has expanded to embrace 27 nations and boasts an economy equal to that of the United States, it is like a man well into middle age whose career accomplishments are behind him.

The EU birthday party was further proof, were any needed, that no transnational institution can elicit the love and loyalty of a country. World Government is a vision of elites no patriot will ever embrace. Men have died in the millions for Poland, France, Italy, England and Germany. Who would walk through fire for the European Union?

What Has the EU Done?

The EU's champions claim its great achievement is to have kept the peace of Europe. "Sixty years of peace means that the image of the EU as a bastion against war is losing its resonance," said Jose Manuel Barroso, head of the European Commission, the executive arm that sits in Brussels [Belgium].

Intending no disrespect to Barroso, it was not the EU that [kept] Europe secure and at peace. America kept the Red Army from the Elbe and the Rhine [rivers bordering Germany]. America saved Western Europe from the fate of the Hungarians in 1956, the Czechs in 1968 and the Poles in 1981. America pulled the British and French chestnuts out of the Balkan fires of the 1990s.

Opinion on UK Immigration

No one would wish to turn away genuine asylum seekers. No one can turn away migrants from the European Union, whether we wish to or not. The result is that we already have far more prospective immigrants than we could hope to accommodate.

The number of genuine asylum seekers is limited and the number of EU migrants, with incontestable rights to settle here, is as good as limitless. Surely it follows that the group that morally or legally has less right to come here is therefore the immigrants who are neither EU nationals nor spouses of Britons.

Minette Marin, Sunday Times *(London), June 17, 2007.*

German-French amity is a product of statesmanship, but also of the defeat of France in 1940 and the reduction of Germany to rubble by the American, British and Soviet armies in 1944–1945.

The 50th anniversary of the EU brought to the fore as many questions as telegrams of congratulations. Quo vadis? Where is Europe going?

Other than commerce, what is the EU all about? Why is Europe so strategically impotent? What happened to the continent that was the cockpit of history?

The Unpopular EU

According to a poll published by the *Washington Times*, not half the citizens of its 27 member states think positively of the EU. Only 28 percent of Brits think well of it. Only a third believes EU membership is good for Great Britain.

After a committee led by ex-President Giscard d'Estaing of France wrote a constitution, setting the EU on course toward a "United States of Europe." France and Holland voted it down. Resentment of the "faceless bureaucrats of Brussels," where the European Commission sits, is rampant.

As the votes in Holland and France show, nationalism is tearing at the aging fabric of European unity. Nor is the EU deeply democratic. Giscard is demanding another vote because, as he says, the French "got it wrong." They must vote again and again, till they get it right. This is the soft tyranny of an elite that knows better than the people what is best for the people.

Many in Europe oppose plans to bring in new members, especially Turkey, an Islamic nation of 70 million, which will soon be more populous than Germany. This raises another issue.

The Immigrant Issue

Not one member of the EU has a birthrate among its native born to enable it to survive in its present form.

Europe's welfare states are failing to produce the babies to replace the aging and shrinking population. Thus, virtually all the nations of Western Europe are undergoing invasions— from the Mahgreb, Middle East, South Asia or sub-Saharan Africa.

Yet, asked if they agree that "immigrants contribute a lot to my country," only 40 percent of EU citizens said, "Yes." Hostility to immigration is strongest in Eastern Europe. Not one in five Hungarians, Czechs, Estonians, Latvians or Slovakians thinks immigration is good for their country. They want to remain who they are, and their country to remain what it has been.

When Chancellor Angela Merkel, hostess of the party, drafted a "birthday card," the Berlin Declaration, even that created dissension and division.

Some nations objected to any mention of the new constitution. Vaclav Havel of the Czech Republic called the declaration "Orwellian Eurospeak." Poland objected to the failure to mention Christianity as birth mother of Europe. Pope Benedict XVI called the failure to credit Christianity an act of "apostasy." The Christophobic [Christianity-fearing] French elite got their way again.

What the malaise of the EU tells us is what patriots have already known. Democracy and free markets are not enough. Dry documents, no matter how eloquent, abstract ideas, no matter how beautiful, do not a nation make. What makes a people and a nation is a unique history and heritage, language and literature, songs and stories, traditions and customs, blood, soil and the mystic chords of memory.

The EU is a thing of paper, an intellectual construct. Unlike a nation, it has no heart and no soul. And if and when it passes into history because of some irreconcilable dispute, many may regret it. Few will weep.

"At least for now, the European Union is merely adrift—not yet about to unravel."

The European Union Needs to Become More Centralized and Define Its Future

Charles Kupchan

In the following viewpoint, Charles Kupchan argues that the European Union is at a critical point in history and urgent action is needed among member states to make the union a priority. Kupchan claims that the four main issues undermining the strength of the union are sovereignty concerns, identity crises, resurgences of nationalism, and generational differences. Charles Kupchan is an associate professor of international relations in the School of Foreign Service and Government Department at Georgetown University in Washington, D.C. He is also a senior fellow and director of Europe Studies at the Council on Foreign Relations.

As you read, consider the following questions:

1. According to Kupchan, what are some of the specific concerns that have made some citizens of European Union member states want to reassert their sovereignty?

Charles Kupchan, "Is the EU Destined to Fail?" *The Globalist*, June 16, 2006. www .theglobalist.com. Reproduced by permission of the author.

47

2. According to the author, what is causing many citizens of European Union member states to feel that their identity is threatened?

3. What historical experience does Kupchan suggest as a source of the generational divide?

During Britain's May 2006 local elections, a Conservative Party long uneasy with integration into Europe routed the Labour Party. Meanwhile, two anti-EU [anti-European Union] parties joined Poland's governing coalition.

A European constitution—rejected last year [2005] by France and Netherlands—is now dead in the water. Economic nationalism and protectionism are surging. The Italian, French, Spanish and Polish governments have taken recent steps to protect national industries from takeover.

On a continent that dreamed of eliminating national borders, hostility toward immigrants—especially those from Muslim countries—is causing national boundaries to spring back to life.

In short, political life across Europe is being re-nationalized, plunging the enterprise of European integration into its most serious crisis since World War II.

Europeans would not be the only losers if the EU continues to stumble. Americans might have to confront the return of national jealousies to Europe—as well as an EU that is too weak to provide the United States the economic and strategic partner it needs.

Concerns About Sovereignty

Four main forces are undermining the EU's foundations. First, Europe's paternalistic welfare states are struggling to survive the dual forces of European integration and globalization.

Citizens are fighting back, insisting that the state reassert its sovereignty against unwelcome forces of change.

Support for the EU

Popular support for the EU has been falling consistently over recent years. Member-states have fed this trend by using the EU as a scapegoat for their own ills and policy failures. Many people have held Europe responsible for the perceived negative impact of globalisation on their daily lives. The EU is viewed as a vehicle for forces such as neo-liberal economics and immigration—even globalisation itself—which many citizens would prefer to keep at bay.

In this difficult political and constitutional—even existential—predicament, the only way forward would be for the EU to find a new sense of direction and show its relevance to its citizens.

Aurore Wanlin, openDemocracy, 2006.

When they voted down the European constitution in 2005, many French citizens blamed the "ultra-liberal" EU for their economic woes. This spring, rioters took to the streets of Paris to block labor reforms. Italians grumble that the euro has depressed their economy.

Especially in France, Germany and Italy, governments are caught in the middle, squeezed from above by the pressures of competitive markets—and from below by an electorate clinging to the comforts of the past and fearful of the uncertainties of the future.

The result is a political stalemate and economic stagnation, which only intensifies the public's discontent and its skepticism of the benefits of European integration.

Immigration and Identity

Second, a combination of the union's enlargement and the influx of Muslim immigrants has diluted traditional European identities and created new social cleavages. The EU now [as of June 2006] has 25 member states at very different levels of development.

Fifteen million Muslims reside within the EU—and Turkey, with 70 million Muslims, is knocking on the membership door. Too many of Europe's Muslims are achingly distant from the social mainstream, their alienation providing inroads for radicalism.

Unaccustomed to multiethnic society and fearful of an Islamist threat from within, the EU's majority populations are retreating behind the illusory comfort of national boundaries and ethnic conceptions of nationhood.

Returning to Nationalism

Third, European politics is growing increasingly populist—not good news for an EU commonly viewed as an elite affair. Voters see both European and national institutions as ineffective and detached.

In France, the far-right National Front is enjoying unprecedented popularity. In a recent survey, one-third called the party in tune with "the concerns of the French people."

Polish voters recently elected a nationalist and protectionist president, Lech Kaczynski, who insists that "what interests the Poles is the future of Poland—and not that of the EU."

A Generational Divide

Finally, Europe is lacking the strong leadership needed to breathe new life into the enterprise of union. Governments in London, Paris, Berlin and Rome are fragile and distracted, preoccupied by the challenges of governing divided and angry electorates.

Generational change is exacerbating matters. For Europeans who lived through World War II and its bitter aftermath, the EU is a sacred antidote to Europe's bloody past.

But this generation is passing from the scene, ceding influence to younger Europeans who have no past from which they seek escape—and no passion for political union.

Action Is Needed

At least for now, the European Union is merely adrift—not yet about to unravel. Furthermore, its demise is hardly inevitable. Over the past six decades, Europe has weathered many periods of self-doubt and stasis.

But only bold and urgent steps can put the union back on track. With the French government in turmoil until at least the 2007 elections, a partnership between Germany and Italy will have to replace the Franco-German coalition as Europe's guiding core.

As a former head of the EU Commission, Italian Prime Minister Romano Prodi has the instincts and expertise, but will have to convince German chancellor Angela Merkel to make Europe a top priority.

European leaders will have to give up the pretense of business as usual—and acknowledge the gravity of the current political crisis.

They should scrap the belabored EU constitution in favor of a leaner document that salvages a few key provisions, such as appointment of an EU president and foreign minister and reform of decision making. Only a more centralized and capable union can make the EU more relevant to the lives of its citizens.

Prodi and Merkel will also have to take the lead in forging a compact that embraces both vital economic reforms and measures to integrate immigrants into the mainstream—steps necessary to improve competitiveness, promote growth and replenish shrinking workforces and pensions.

Europeans must face the reality that they have reached a watershed moment. Unless they urgently revive the project of political and economic union, one of the greatest accomplishments of the 20th century will be at risk.

Periodical Bibliography

The following articles have been selected to supplement the diverse views presented in this chapter.

BBC News   "Q & A: EU Constitution's Future," June 22, 2007.

Helle Dale   "Pushing Paper: New EU Treaty, but Same Ideas and Sentiment," *Washington Times*, October 24, 2007.

The Economist   "Trick or Treaty?" June 28, 2007.

William Kristol   "A New Europe?" *The Weekly Standard*, June 6, 2005.

Donald Lambro   "What's Next for EU . . . and U.S.?" *Washington Times*, June 6, 2005.

Paul Magnette   "European Governance and Civic Participation: Beyond Elitist Citizenship?" *Political Studies*, March 2003.

Minette Marrin   "Should We Limit Immigrants to Europeans?" *Sunday Times* (London), June 17, 2007.

Carol Matlack   "Stars of Europe: 25 Leaders at the Forefront of Change," *Business Week*, May 30, 2005.

Andrew Moravcsik   "A Too Perfect Union? Why Europe Said 'No,'" *Current History*, November 2005.

Aurore Wanlin   "Adieu, Europe?" *openDemocracy.net*, June 29, 2006. www.opendemocracy.net/democracy-eu rope_constitution/adieu_3694.jsp.

Steve Watson   "EU Federal Superstate Becoming a Reality: European Globalists No Longer Even Pretend the People Will Have a Say," *Infowars.net*, April 18, 2007. www.infowars.net/articles/april2007/180407EU.htm.

CHAPTER 2

What Countries Should Be Members of the European Union?

Chapter Preface

The prelude to the European Union (EU) came just after the end of World War II, when the six original member countries created one European Coal and Steel Community in 1952. The impetus for this was both economic and political. The desire for peace was strong at this point in history; forming an alliance around the commodities of coal and steel helped contribute to a future of peace among these countries. To this day peace is still often cited as a reason for European countries to unite to form a political and economic union.

The European Commission, the European Union's executive institution, claims that "war between EU countries is now unthinkable, thanks to the unity that has been built up between them over the last 50 years." The economic prosperity created by the European Union is not seen as a separate benefit but part of what creates peace in the first place, with economic stability helping to guarantee political stability. The European Commission states that the European Union now exists as a model for other parts of the world since it "shows how democratic countries can successfully pool economic and political resources in the common interest."

Besides acting as a model for more distant parts of the world, the ability to forge peace through accession into the union is one of the reasons given for the EU to expand. As of 2007, candidate countries to the European Union include Croatia, Turkey, and the former Yugoslav Republic of Macedonia. The European Union is looking at further enlistments in the Western Balkans, including Albania, Bosnia and Herzegovina, Montenegro, and Serbia. The Socialist Federal Republic of Yugoslavia dissolved in 1992 amid the Yugoslav wars, but the European Union may one day bring the six republics back together in a different way: Slovenia became a member in 2004; Croatia and Macedonia are currently candidate countries; and the remaining three republics (Bosnia and Herzegovina, Montenegro, and Serbia) have a good chance of becoming candidate countries in the future.

While there certainly are other reasons for countries to form a union and for existing unions to allow for further enlargements, peace will always be a top concern. In the following chapter, the authors debate an important question for current members and would-be members: What Countries Should Be Members of the European Union?

> *"It is inevitable that the EU will continue to grow and find its finality in a pan-European coalition of 40+ Member States."*

The European Union Will Continue to Expand

Hans-Juergen Zahorka

In the following viewpoint, Hans-Juergen Zahorka argues that the European Union (EU) will continue to expand, given the advantages of membership. Zahorka believes that people are starting to recognize the advantages of a larger EU. Zahorka explains the current ties between the EU and nearby countries, giving his views on the likely accession of such countries. Hans-Juergen Zahorka is director of LIBERTAS European Institute, a German-based think tank focusing on European and international economy and policy. Formerly a member of European Parliament, Zahorka teaches European Affairs at various universities and graduate schools.

As you read, consider the following questions:

1. What is the ambiguity, according to the author, of the meaning of "European state" within the EU Treaty?

Hans-Juergen Zahorka, "How Far Should the European Union Reach?" *GALAxy Newsletter*, 2006 (updated January 2008). www.gala-global.org/GALAxy-article-how _far_should_the_european_union_reach-4107.html. Reproduced by permission of the publisher and author.

2. According to Zahorka, what kind of relationship does Switzerland have with the EU?

3. What is the relationship between the countries of the former Soviet Union and the European Union, according to the author?

One of the most frequently discussed questions in globalising business is how far the European Union Single Market should reach. Companies want to expand, to open subsidiaries, and to cooperate with local partners; not only for mere expansion, but also because they want to be active on a regional or global scale.

The question concerning the outreach of the Single Market often focuses on investment security and non-discrimination, as well as on basic rules of jurisdiction in trade and commerce. Transnational companies of all sizes often have regional offices in foreign markets, which makes it desirable to set up offices in other regions under the safe umbrella of the Single Market (i.e. a French company sets up an office in Romania for the whole Black Sea region).

How far will the Single Market, that is, the European Union, reach? I think—and many of my think-tank colleagues also believe—that it is inevitable that the EU will continue to grow and find its finality in a pan-European coalition of 40+ Member States. This is contested by some politicians and by many "ordinary people", but the more information and background available, the more people are in favour of this vision.

One of the "soft powers" of the EU is to attract other countries into its periphery, due to the uncontested economic advantages of belonging to the Single Market and being stabilized politically by being part of the EU. However, it is clear that any further enlargement of the European Union needs a kind of "streamlining" of its internal organisation. A kind of constitutional arrangement in the direction of the Constitution (ratified in May/June 2005 by about two-thirds of Member States, but not by France and the Netherlands in their referendums) was urgently needed for any further development in the EU. It was always certain that these constitution-like rules would come. In June 2007 the European Council (heads of state and governments) agreed on the basics of a so-called Reform Treaty which was adopted in the successor meeting in December 2007. Members have until January 1, 2009 to ratify it, and there a referendum will be held in Ireland only. The ratification process is underway in all the Member States.

The Accession Process

According to the present EU Treaty (art. 49), which has not been changed by the Reform Treaty, each European state can apply for EU accession. It is not clearly defined if this means European "state" according to geographic criteria or "European-minded" state. Between these extremes, a compromise can and will be found. European states can be those of the Council of Europe, which comprises member states of "Greater Europe", some of which are partly on territories considered Asian (like Turkey, Russia, and the Caucasus countries). With the pan-European vision of the present EU, there is a leaning in this direction. The EU (with at present 27 Member States) and the Council of Europe (an international organisation like the Organization of American States; with 47 Member States, all European democracies, with the exception of Belarus) have also to cooperate very closely; this is the reason why many European sources say that Member States of the Council of Europe have, in principle, the right to apply for membership of the EU.

An application has to be directed to the Council of the European Union (the council of the governments of the Member States), and then must be evaluated by the EU Commission (which is the supranational "government" of the EU). This comes as a "Regular Report" every year. The current negotiations are also run by the Commission, which elaborates an Accession Treaty with the acceding Member State. This has to be approved by the European Parliament (with the absolute majority of its members) and by the Council, which has to unanimously approve this treaty. Furthermore it will have to be ratified by the Member States and the relevant acceding state. It is evident that these hurdles are now more difficult to overcome, with 27 Member States, than in former times, with six or nine.

The "Copenhague Criteria" were added 1993, when the latest round of enlargements by the Central and Eastern European states took place. These criteria signalled a clear "yes" to a market economy system, to active participation in the competition of the EU, to a pluralist democracy, human rights, minorities' protection, and the general rule of law. And they mean a "yes" to the takeover of the whole *acquis communautaire*, the whole set of rules instituted until now, including some 80,000 pages of EU Laws (most of which concern agricultural law), but also the European Monetary Union (the Euro). That means that new Member States do not have to have the same economic strength as existing ones. But the threshold of sustainable development into the direction of the "average EU" must be passed. This is undoubtedly a political decision.

The EU never uses any force—in the sense of economic or psychological force—on any state to become a member. However, the EU exercises objectively a centrifugal or "suck-in" effect on countries in its topical periphery. This happens because of the effect of the EU Single Market, which has proven to be very attractive.

The present EU wins a new international, geopolitical weight with the addition of every new Member State. To create a "Common Foreign and Defense Policy" is an important task for the near future. Beginning January 1, 2009, the EU will have a Vice President of the EU Commission, who will

Accession Criteria

In 1993, at the Copenhagen European Council, the [European] Union took a decisive step towards the fifth enlargement, agreeing that "the associated countries in Central and Eastern Europe that so desire shall become members of the European Union." Thus, enlargement was no longer a question of 'if', but 'when'.

Concerning the timing, the European Council states: "Accession will take place as soon as an associated country is able to assume the obligations of membership by satisfying the economic and political conditions required." At the same time, it defined the membership criteria, which are often referred to as the 'Copenhagen criteria'.

Membership criteria require that the candidate country must have achieved

- stability of institutions guaranteeing democracy, the rule of law, human rights and respect for and protection of minorities;

- the existence of a functioning market economy as well as the capacity to cope with competitive pressure and market forces within the Union;

- the ability to take on the obligations of membership including adherence to the aims of political, economic & monetary union.

European Commission, "Accession Criteria."
http://ec.europa.eu.

act as a kind of Foreign Minister of the present 27 Member States, with a diplomatic service of its own.

Regardless of a country's economic system, the negotiations last between eight and eleven years, on average. The negotiations with Austria, Finland, and Sweden before 1995 were so short because all three countries were already in the Single Market—the core of the EU—being members of the EEA (European Economic Area: the EU Single Market plus EFTA countries, minus Switzerland, who had voted against being in the EEA).

The EU Relationship with Peripheral Countries

The EU has the following system of external relations within its (European) periphery:

- European Economic Area (EEA): this includes Norway, Iceland and Liechtenstein. All these countries might end up in the EU, but at present no major policy moves are visible. A large percentage of Norway's population doesn't favor the EU, as joining would mean shortening the yearly farm subventions by 2/3. Iceland's economy is dependent on fishing, which is covered by the Common Agricultural Policy, and Liechtenstein will do what Switzerland does. However, the Norwegian government is waiting for a favourable situation to reverse the negative polls of the past, and in Iceland for the first time a parliamentary committee has been set up to examine the pros and cons of a possible EU membership.

- Bilateral Agreements: with Switzerland only. Switzerland plays a special role: although the majority of its population is not ready to join the EU, it is surrounded by EU Member States, which are involved in its economy to a very large extent. Switzerland will also take part in the free circulation of citizens as provided by the Schengen Agreement (abolition of passport controls at the EU borders).

- European Agreements (EA): for the ten states which have become members since May 2004 (Estonia, Latvia,

Lithuania, Poland, Czech Republic, Slovak Republic, Hungary, Slovenia, Cyprus and Malta), as well as Romania and Bulgaria (who joined January 1, 2007). However, in some of these new Member States, some homework must be finished (anti-corruption measures, streamlining of the justice system etc.), but all the states see the objective need to fulfil these requirements. The EAs were individual and far-reaching association agreements permitting asymmetrical market access, according to the degree of progress in establishing democracy and market economy, which finally led to membership.

- Stabilisation and Association Agreements (SAA): for the West Balkan states (Croatia; Macedonia; Serbia, the new state of Montenegro; Kosovo, which most likely will be a more or less independent state in 1-2 years; Bosnia-Herzegovina; and Albania). Similar to the EAs, the SAAs also offer a membership vision, which may occur between 2015 and 2020. But it's up to these countries to change their policies (e.g. towards the International Court of War Crimes in The Hague) and approximate their legislation. These countries comprise about 4.5% of the EU population (22 of 460 million), but 26% of the number of Member States (7 of 27)—it is evident that this is manageable only with a new constitution-like legal framework of the EU. Although it is not too popular to talk about this now, these countries will have to be inserted into the EU for economic and social reasons, but also for political reasons; another Srebrenica or Kosovo war is unthinkable and can be avoided only within a European Union.

- Turkey applied for membership in 1996, after having concluded an Association Treaty with the EU in 1963. Modern Turkey, to which a further reform policy will gradually lead, will enlarge considerably the foreign-policy influence of the whole EU in the Middle East, Central Asia, and the Islamic world. Discussions about Turkey's possible membership are often influenced by old impressions or modern voices which are sometimes nationalistic. The EU has a non-nationalist structure, and this problem will hopefully be solved in a generation. But today Turkey is already very much oriented towards the EU in economic terms, and has had a common external customs tariff with the EU for many years. If Turkey's development proceeds in a linear way, it will be ready for EU membership in approximately fifteen years, perhaps with some additonal transition time.

- The EU has Partnership and Cooperation Agreements (PCA) with the successor states of the former Soviet Union: Russia, Ukraine, Moldova, Georgia, Armenia, Azerbaijan, Kazakhstan, Kyrgyzstan, Tajikistan, Uzbekistan and Turkmenistan. There is also a PCA with Belarus, but it is de facto frozen now, due to the nature of the leader of this country.

- Russia is unlikely to join the EU for several reasons. But Ukraine, Moldova and Georgia have already expressed their interest, though knowing that they have to do their homework. The EU provides assistance by financing know-how and structural reforms. Armenia also wants to approach to the EU; they will soon establish a Ministry of European Integration, and, since the last parliamentary election, the Parliamentary Committee on European Integration is permanent and no longer a sub-committee. Some (advanced) think-tanks in the EU have already made models for EU troops in Nagorny-Karabakh, the region contested between Armenia and Azerbaijan. The PCAs, however, have no

Membership vision as such; they were concluded in the mid-'90s and have now to be renegotiated and renewed.

- Since the last enlargement in May 2004, the EU has followed a new policy toward the "ring of friends" in the new periphery, called the European Neighbourhood Policy (ENP). It applies to all the European CIS countries (Ukraine, Moldova, Georgia, Armenia and Azerbaijan, as well as Belarus (which has not really started) and Russia (which has no ENP as such, but has four "Common European Spaces" on economy, research, and internal and external security), but also to Northern Africa (Morocco, Algeria, Tunisia, Libya and Egypt) and the Middle East (Jordan, Syria, Lebanon, Israel and the Palestine Authority). Besides the CIS-stemming countries, which have an enlarged interest in EU accession, none of the other countries has spoken in favour of EU accession, although there have been some voices in Israel and Tunisia. But the EU wants a very wide and open exchange of goods, services, investment, and culture, and it wants its values to be practiced in its neighbourhood—a long road ahead!

- There is a second "ring of friends", which is being slowly but surely attracted by the EU economy: the Sahel zone states in Africa (Mauritania, Senegal, Mali, Niger, Tchad, maybe Sudan and Somalia); the Arab peninsula (Saudi Arabia, Yemen); the Gulf states (maybe even Iraq and Iran); the East of Russia, Central Asia; Kazakhstan, which has more than 150,000 square kilometers within Europe; Kyrgyzstan; Uzbekistan; Tajikistan; and Turkmenistan. The EU has no interest at all in any unstable development of these states, and it can be assumed that a kind of "European Neighbourhood Policy plus" will be launched in the coming years—maybe under other names. This of course does not concern any new memberships, but it is interesting to discuss with some intellectuals in these countries, as they often hypothetically discuss the membership of their countries.

The European micro states (Andorra, San Marino, and Monaco) will not be in the EU—we need some spots where old independent or royal states can exist, be they as small as those. In the Vatican, the equality standards between men and women at the workplace will inevitably fail. In Switzerland, the Bilateral Agreements have eliminated the pressure, but in the period beginning in 2010, it is not impossible that the EU will play a big role again—and this time a decisive one. Whatever will come, Europe's landscape has changed very fast during the last years, and the future is thrilling, including the necessary discussions about the EU's internal structure before further major enlargements.

> *"Both existing and wannabe members'*
> *doubts about further enlargement will*
> *grow in the coming years."*

The European Union Faces Hurdles to Continued Expansion

The Economist

In the following viewpoint, the Economist *argues that future expansion of the European Union (EU) will prove challenging. Among the various theories of expansion, the author prefers the hypothesis that the EU will reach a stable size in the near future that will preclude new members. In support of this, the author cites various reasons why potential new members face unique challenges to accession. The* Economist *is a weekly magazine offering analysis and opinion on business and political events.*

As you read, consider the following questions:

1. What are the three theories the author cites regarding future expansion of the European Union?

2. According to the author, what countries face problems in being defined as "European"?

3. What barrier do countries aspiring to join the European Union have in common, according to the author?

There are worries that a European Union of 25 member countries [as of 2004] will prove unmanageable. But the queue to join continues growing. Could the Union one day expand to take in the whole of continental Europe and beyond?

Rather like the various theories of the universe, it is possible to imagine a European Union [EU] that goes on expanding, one that reaches a certain size then remains stable, or one that eventually implodes. So far, the EU continues in its expansionary phase. On Saturday, May 1st [2004] it undergoes its fifth and most ambitious enlargement since its foundation, as the European Economic Community, in 1957. The EU aims to admit Romania and Bulgaria in 2007, and Croatia may also join around then.

Already, there are worries that the current enlargement will prove a step too far. Getting agreement between 25 squabbling countries may prove near-impossible. There are also fears that mass migration from the poorer eastern entrants will cause a backlash against the EU among richer existing members. Already, EU citizens have doubts about the European project: a poll last December [2003] by Eurobarometer found that fewer than half of its people now agree that the Union is "a good thing".

However, while fears of the Union falling apart are growing, so is the queue of aspiring members—and not just among countries that geographers would call European. Israel and Morocco would both like to join. If they get in, why not Algeria, which held a reasonably democratic election in early April [2004]—and which belonged to France, and thus to the EU's predecessor body, until the 1960s? Or Tunisia, the first North African country to sign an association agreement with the EU?

Opinions on Whether the EU Should Expand					
Great Britain %	France %	Italy %	Spain %	Germany %	United States %
Yes 29	20	48	35	33	46
No 47	67	41	40	55	5
Not Sure 23	13	11	25	12	49

Base: All EU adults in five countries and US adults
Note: Percentages may not add up to 100% due to rounding

TAKEN FROM: *The Harris Poll®*, June 20, 2007.

Requirements for Joining the EU

After the fall of the Berlin Wall in 1989 [an event symbolizing unification between democratic and communist factions] led to a rush of applications from countries previously behind the [communist] Iron Curtain, the EU refined its entry requirements. Under the "Copenhagen criteria", agreed in 1993, applicants must be stable democracies that guarantee the rule of law and human rights; they must have a functioning market economy; and they must be capable of taking on all the obligations of EU membership, including its colossal body of existing laws (known as the *acquis communautaine*).

There is one other stipulation in the EU's treaties: members should be "European". But the meaning of this is not defined. Turkey has had its application formally recognised, despite most of its territory being in Asia. Georgia would like to join, but while geographers place it in Europe, it is actually to the east of Syria and Jordan. Azebaijan is also geographically European but its chances of ever being accepted seem remote. Nevertheless, Mikhail Saakashvili, Georgia's president, predicts that all the countries in the Caucasus will eventually join.

Some would argue that "European" means culturally European—including being predominantly Christian. But the EU has ruled out discriminating on religious grounds, by acknowledging Turkey's application and by making it clear that Bosnia—also predominantly Muslim—will one day have its application considered, as will the other Balkan states if they continue making progress towards the Copenhagen criteria.

If all of southern Europe can apply, why not all of eastern Europe? Maybe one day but, as Heather Grabbe of the Centre for European Reform puts it, "Belarus is too authoritarian, Moldova too poor, Ukraine too large and Russia too scary for the EU to contemplate offering membership any time soon." The EU's single-market commissioner, Frits Bolkestein, argues in a new book that these four countries should be permanently ruled out (he thinks Turkey should be, too). It is a good job that they are all a long way from fulfilling the Copenhagen criteria because the cost of incorporating them would be enormous.

The Problem with Possible New Members

There are several small, prosperous, western European states that the EU would welcome with open arms: Norway and Switzerland (whose governments have contemplated joining but whose citizens voted against) plus Iceland and micro-states such as Jersey, Liechtenstein and Monaco. These all have relationships with the EU offering them most of the benefits of membership while sparing them some of its obligations, so they are under no great pressure to join.

The countries that do want to join are mostly poor. What most attracts them are the big EU subsidies that helped lift earlier joiners, such as Spain and Ireland, from rags to riches. But the generosity of the EU's wealthier paymasters is already under great strain and would reach breaking-point if more impoverished countries joined on the same terms as past entrants.

This problem is compounded by the size of some of the poor, would-be members: Turkey could be the Union's most populous member by the time it is ready to join, in about

2015. This would upset the current balance of power, in which the biggest countries (and thus those with the most votes) have been the main paymasters. In the biggest and richest current member, Germany, the opposition Christian Democrats, who oppose Turkish membership, could quite easily return to power in the 2006 elections.

The arguments that the EU's leaders have used to justify enlargement—that it will make Europe a region of prosperity and peace, and that it will further the Union's aim of becoming a global power—could justify its expanding to encompass the whole continent and beyond. But both existing and wannabe members' doubts about further enlargement will grow in the coming years, especially as the latest entrants struggle to implement tough EU rules, without the generous subsidies of the past to oil the wheels of integration. As the Union gets bigger, Brussels may come to be seen as remote and dictatorial. The waning attractions of full EU membership may eventually persuade some applicants to accept the alternative the Union offered them last year: under the "Wider Europe" initiative, the EU's neighbours will get free trade and other benefits in return for political and economic reforms. If so, the steady-state theory of the EU may eventually prove correct.

*"I cannot believe in a Europe without a
Turkish prospect."*

Turkey Should Be Allowed to Join the European Union

Orhan Pamuk

*In the following viewpoint, Orhan Pamuk argues that Turkey
should be allowed to join the European Union (EU). Pamuk expresses his concern about public opinion within the EU regarding Turkey's bid for accession, asserting that anti-Turkish sentiment and European nationalism are closely linked. Nationalistic
sentiment, he claims, is dangerous both for Europe and for Turkey. Pamuk claims that the Turkish people have something very
important to offer Europe by joining the EU. Orhan Pamuk is a
Turkish novelist who was awarded the 2006 Nobel Prize for Literature.*

As you read, consider the following questions:

1. How has Turkey's bid to become a member of the European Union affected European sentiment about Turkey,
   according to Pamuk?

2. According to the author, what is the most important thing that Turkey and the Turkish people have to offer the European Union?

3. What does the author suggest is the primary sentiment in Turkey regarding accession into the European Union?

I grew up in a house where everyone read novels. My father had a large library, and when I was a child, my father would discuss the great novelists—[Thomas] Mann, [Franz] Kafka, [Fyodor] Dostoyevsky and [Leo] Tolstoy—the way other fathers discussed famous generals and saints. From an early age, all these novelists—these great novelists—were linked in my mind with the idea of Europe. But this is not just because I came from an Istanbul [Turkey] family that believed fervently in Westernization, and therefore longed, in its innocence, to believe itself and its country far more Western than they really were. It was also because the novel was one of the greatest artistic achievements to come out of Europe. The novel, like orchestral music and post-Renaissance painting, is in my opinion one of the cornerstones of European civilization; it is what makes Europe what it is, the means by which Europe has created and made visible its nature, if there is such a thing. I cannot think of Europe without novels.

I am speaking now of the novel as a way of thinking, understanding and imagining, and also as a way of imagining oneself as someone else. In other parts of the world, children and young people first meet Europe in depth with their first ventures into novels: I was one of them. To pick up a novel and step inside Europe's borders, to enter a new continent, a new culture, a new civilization—to learn, in the course of these novel explorations, to express oneself with new desire and new inspiration, and to believe, as a consequence, that one was part of Europe—this is how I remember feeling. And let us also remember that the great Russian novel, and the Latin American novel, also stem from European culture—so just to read a novel is to prove that Europe's borders, histories

The Benefit of Turkey in the EU

The prospect of EU membership has pushed Turkey forward, giving a huge incentive for domestic reforms. Turkey's membership would also be a crucial step for the EU, substantially extending its geographic and demographic zone of peace, prosperity and liberty. It would also help thwart the efforts of those who wish to transform predictions of a clash of civilizations into a poisonous reality.

Hakan Altinay and Aryeh Neier,
International Herald Tribune, *May 7, 2004.*

and national distinctions are in constant flux. The old Europe described in the French, Russian and German novels in my father's library is, like the postwar Europe of my own childhood and the Europe of today, a place that is forever changing, and so, too, is our understanding of what Europe means. However, I have one vision of Europe that is constant, and that is what I shall speak of now.

European Sentiment About Turkey

Let me begin by saying that Europe is a very delicate, very sensitive question for a Turk. Here we are, knocking on your door and asking to come in, full of high hopes and good intentions, but also feeling rather anxious and fearing rejection. I feel such things as keenly as other Turks. As Turkey knocks on Europe's door, as we wait and wait, and Europe makes us promises and then forgets us, only to raise the bar—and as Europe examines the full implications of Turkey's bid to become a full member, we've seen lamentable hardening of anti-Turkish sentiment in certain parts of Europe, at least among certain politicians. In the recent elections, when certain politicians took a political line against Turks and Turkey, I found their style just as dangerous as the political style adopted by certain politicians in my own country. It is one thing to criticize the deficiencies of the Turkish state vis-à-vis democracy, or to find fault with its economy; it is quite another to denigrate all of Turkish culture, or those of Turkish descent here in Germany whose lives are among the most difficult and impoverished in the country. As for Turks in Turkey—when they hear themselves judged so cruelly, they are reminded yet again that they are knocking on a door and waiting to be let in, and of course they feel unwelcome. The cruelest irony of all is that the fanning of nationalist anti-Turkish sentiment in Europe has provoked the coarsest of nationalist backlash inside Turkey. Those who believe in the European Union [EU] must see at once that the real choice we have to make is between peace and nationalism. Either we have peace, or we have nationalism. I think that the ideal of peace sits at the heart of the European Union and I believe that the chance of peace that Turkey has offered Europe will not, in the end, be spurned. We've arrived at a point where we must choose between the power of a novelist's imagination and the sort of nationalism that condones burning his books.

What Turkey Can Offer the EU

Over the past few years, I have spoken a great deal about Turkey and its EU bid; often I've been met with grimaces and suspicious questions. So let me answer them here and now. The most important thing that Turkey and the Turkish people have to offer Europe and Germany is, without a doubt, peace; it is the security and strength that will come from a Muslim country's desire to join Europe, and this peaceful desire's ratification. The great novelists I read as a child and a young man did not define Europe by its Christian faith but by its individuals. It was because they described Europe through heroes who were struggling to free themselves, express their creativity and make their dreams come true that their novels spoke to my heart. Europe has gained the respect of the non-Western world for the ideals it has done so much to nurture: liberty, equality and fraternity. If Europe's soul is enlightenment, equality and democracy, if it is to be a union predicated on peace, then Turkey has a place in it. A Europe defining itself on narrow Christian terms will, like a Turkey that tries to derive its strength only from its religion, be an inward-looking place divorced from reality, and more bound to the past than to the future.

Having grown up in a Westernized secular family in the European part of Istanbul, it is not at all difficult for me—or people like me—to believe in the European Union. Don't forget, since childhood my football team, Fenerbahçe, has been playing in the European Cup. There are millions of Turks like me, who believe heart and soul in the European Union. But what is more important is that most of today's conservative and Muslim Turks, and with them their political representatives, want to see Turkey in the European Union, help to plan Europe's future, dreaming it into being and helping to build it. Coming as it does after centuries of war and conflict, this gesture of friendship cannot be taken lightly, and to reject it outright would be cause for huge regret. Just as I cannot imagine a Turkey without a European prospect, I cannot believe in a Europe without a Turkish prospect.

"Turkish membership would be bad for the Union."

Turkey Should Not Be Allowed to Join the European Union

Tom Spencer

In the following viewpoint, Tom Spencer argues that Turkey should not be permitted to join the European Union (EU). Spencer claims that the arguments in favor of Turkey's accession are weak. He believes the focus should be on integrating southeast Europe rather than on enlarging the EU to include Turkey. Spencer points to Turkey's history with Europe as an important reason to deny that nation entrance to the EU. Tom Spencer is executive director of the European Centre for Public Affairs and visiting professor of public affairs at Brunel University in Uxbridge, England.

As you read, consider the following questions:

1. Why does Spencer deny that the reason the European Union has refused thus far to admit Turkey is because Turkey is primarily a Muslim state?

Tom Spencer, "Good Reasons for Saying No to Turkey," European Centre for Public Affairs, August 19, 2004. www.publicaffairs.ac/articles/NoToTurkey.pdf. Reproduced by permission of the author.

2. Why does the author argue that the European Union should expend its political energies completing the unification of Europe, rather than enlarging Europe to include Turkey?

3. What historical event does Spencer identify in support of the view that history is relevant to denying Turkey entrance into the EU?

The division between Europe and Asia goes back to 220 BC when [mapmaker] Eratosthenes wrote 'Europe' to the west of the Bosporus and 'Asia' to its east. In the nineteenth century geographers and historians were very clear. They divided the Ottoman Empire into Turkey in Europe and Asia Minor. All that remains of Turkey in Europe is the toe of land flanking Istanbul. To argue that this makes Turkey a European nation in geographical terms is flimsy. Is Spain an African nation because of its enclaves on the North African coast? If Gibraltar belonged to Morocco rather than Britain, would we have said yes to Morocco's application to join the European Union? One could of course argue that Turkey should not be the only geographically non-European member of the European Union [EU] and that Morocco and Armenia would make excellent candidates. But if Morocco, why not Algeria? If Armenia, why not Azerbaijan? The Treaty definition requiring candidates to be European would have been exposed to "mission creep" of the most flagrant kind. Timothy Garton Ash, while arguing the case for Turkish membership, does admit that he would "hate to plead the case in any historian's court that Morocco is not a European country, but Turkey is".

Bad Arguments for Turkey's Joining

The truth is that geography is being abused by people with other agendas. It is not a valid argument that the EU should admit Turkey because the Americans want us to, or because Turkey is an important ally of the Israelis. The original American argument about the importance of Turkey in NATO [North Atlantic Treaty Organization] collapsed along with the Soviet Union. In any case the European Union is not NATO, however close the two institutions may become. Both NATO and the Union have changed beyond all recognition since Turkey first sought Associate Membership of the Common Market. American analysts of the euro-phobic school make no secret of their desire for the European Union to be distracted from its global agenda by the problems of absorbing a new country, which would have the population of Germany by the time it joined.

It has become fashionable to denounce those who oppose Turkish membership as wanting to keep Europe as a 'Christian club'. This is to vulgarise thirteen centuries of complex interaction between Europe and Islam. In any case there are already somewhere between twelve and thirteen million Muslims living in the Europe of 25 [as of 2004]. There are a further seven million Muslims in Balkan states. Indeed one might reasonably expect there to be three predominately Muslim states in the completed European Union—Albania, Kosovo and the rump of Bosnia Herzegovina. It is nonsense to say therefore that the European Union refuses to admit Turkey because the predominant religion of its citizens is Islam. What matters much more is the nature of the historical experience and mind-set of the nations which make up Europe.

Priorities of the EU

The admission of Turkey to the Union would take up political energies that should more properly be used in completing the unification of Europe by admitting the states of South Eastern Europe with their predominately Orthodox tradition. The Emperor Diocletian's split is still visible in the order in which we are admitting East and Central Europe to the Union: Catholic and Protestant states first. The American strategist Thomas Barnett has an elegant model dividing the world into

the Core, which has accepted globalisation, and a Gap which remains resistant to globalisation and covers much of the Arab world and Sub-Saharan African. He points out that the most interesting recent development is the enlargement of the Core by countries such as Russia, China and India. One can draw a similar model for the European Union where the original Core has been joined by the states of the recent enlargement, but where many of the countries of South East Europe display the Gap-like characteristics of failed or failing states. Europe's most pressing mission should be to close this 'Balkan Gap' with its attendant violence and criminal activity.

A new variant of the case for admitting Turkey stresses the supposed need to balance Europe's ageing population with a vast import of predominantly Islamic young labour. Barnett argues that the USA will meet its own ageing problem in its traditional way by admitting millions of migrants from Mexico and Latin America. He calculates that to achieve the same 'success', the European Union would need to admit 1.5 million immigrants a year and that by 2050 a quarter of its population would be foreign born. However the world is moving towards population balance or indeed reduction by 2050, so such vast upheavals would only 'solve' the ageing problem for one generation. One is surely entitled to wonder by what right Muslim immigration is privileged over non-Muslim? Similarly, one might wonder why Turkish Muslims are privileged over Egyptian or Indian Muslim immigrants?

In truth there is a great deal of sloppy and self-serving analysis around. Some political parties fear the loss of political support from existing Muslim communities in Europe. Some point to the real, if limited, improvements in Turkish human rights and the suspension of capital punishment, as gains from Europe's application of the Copenhagen Criteria, but surely such things should be welcomed as shared values rather than reluctantly arm-twisted into existence by EU negotiators?

The Importance of History

Underlying the whole question of Turkish membership is the broader mixture of amnesia and self-deception which characterises Europe's induced memories of its long interaction with Islam. Political correctness now requires Europeans to apologise for the Crusades, ignoring the fact that Byzantium had been resisting Islamic pressure for the previous three centuries. This Frankish-centric guilt forgets the Dhilli, the millions of Arab Christians and Jews forcibly converted at sword point in the early centuries of Islam. Behind the sloppy history there lies an implied artificial choice between a "Eurarabia", in which Europe effectively merges its identity with the Arab world to its south, or a "Eurussia" in which an anti-Islamic Europe makes common cause with All The Russias. I find both options unattractive. They ignore Europe's aspiration for unity and democracy, based on shared historical experience. What needs to be explored properly is the much simpler option of a genuinely United Europe, learning to live both with Russia to its east and the Arab world to its south.

I have no doubt therefore that Turkish membership would be bad for the Union. It would also be bad for the Islamic world, which desperately needs examples of successfully functioning democracies. It would send entirely the wrong message if Turkey's recent relative success with democracy was 'rewarded' by its being defined as 'European'. In fact non-Arab Muslim countries have a reasonable history of establishing and preserving democratic regimes. The problem for the Arab world lies in the lack of legitimacy of the regimes which succeeded the destruction of the Ottoman Empire by the British and the French after the First World War. Europe can and should play a key role in bringing security and prosperity to the Greater Middle East. It will not however do so successfully on the basis of sloppy history and poorly defined foreign policy goals. It would be much better to end a generation of diplomatic dishonesty by giving the Turks a simple 'No' now and starting work on the creative task of how Turkey and Europe together can bring security to the regions which they jointly abut.

> *"The only way that England will be saved will be for the English to insist that England leaves the EU."*

Great Britain Should Leave the European Union

Vernon Coleman

In the following viewpoint, Vernon Coleman argues that England should leave the European Union (EU). Coleman bases his argument on his belief that the nation of England is being destroyed and that the English identity is disappearing. Vernon Coleman is a writer and columnist and is author of the book, The Truth They Won't Tell You (and Don't Want You to Know) About the EU.

As you read, consider the following questions:

1. According to Coleman, why is England losing its status as a country?

2. What voice did the English people have regarding the establishment of regional assemblies, according to the author?

3. For what reasons does Coleman believe the English identity is disappearing?

Vernon Coleman, "England Must Leave the EU and Declare Independence If It Is to Have a Chance of Surviving," VernonColeman.com, November 16, 2006. Reproduced by permission.

England is about to disappear. It already no longer exists except as a memory. England was the only team in the recent football World Cup [2006] which didn't represent a nation state.

Look up England in the Encyclopedia Britannica and you'll find these words: 'Despite the political, economic, and cultural legacy that has perpetuated its name ... England no longer officially exists as a country.'

As citizens, all that we inherit of real value is our cultural and spiritual heritage. And yet the English are now almost the only ethnic group in the world to have been deprived of their identity without a gun being fired. The denial of England, and Englishness, is turning the English into stateless persons. It is silent, bloodless ethnic cleansing. It's no exaggeration to say that it's genocide without the blood.

England Is Being Destroyed

The basic reason for this is simple.

The EU [European Union] intends to turn the United Kingdom [UK] into 12 regions. Scotland, Wales and Northern Ireland will still exist as identified regions—though their so-called Parliaments are, in reality, merely Regional Assemblies of the European Union.

England, on the other hand, is being split up into nine regions. Each already has a Regional Assembly—under the authority of Brussels [Belgium, headquarters of the executive arm of the EU]. Eight of the Regional Assemblies are entirely unelected. The members are appointed by the Labour Government. The ninth Regional Assembly is better known as the London Assembly—under Ken Livingstone. It's the only one of the nine which has members who have been elected.

All nine Regional Assemblies were set up under the Regional Development Agencies Act 1998. Their names are:

London Assembly

East of England Regional Assembly

East Midlands Regional Assembly

North East Assembly

North West Regional Assembly

South East England Regional Assembly

South West Regional Assembly

West Midlands Regional Assembly

Yorkshire and Humber Assembly

Voters Ignored

In 2002, [British prime minister Tony] Blair's Government published a White paper called 'Your Region, Your Choice'. They announced that they would allow the voters in each region to approve of the Regional Assemblies they'd all got. But the Government got cold feet and only went ahead with one vote. It was a disaster for the Government and the European Union. In November 2004, the people of the North East— who thought they were deciding whether or not to have a Regional Assembly—rejected the idea by 696,519 votes to 197,310. What they didn't realise was that they'd already got what they'd rejected.

But despite this clear rejection of the idea, all eight unelected Regional Assemblies—including the North East—are still in place. And they are the regional representatives of the European Union. These utterly unelected and undemocratic bodies make very real decisions about how our lives are run. That's all we know. The whole thing is very secretive.

You can, however, find the addresses through the Internet. And you can find signs of their existence through occasional job advertisements in the *Guardian*. For example, just a few minutes ago I found that the North East Assembly is advertising for a Sustainability Manager at £40,000 a year 'to work closely with local authorities and key partner organisations within the Region, to develop all aspects of this work, respond to consultations, lobby for changes and commission research.'

Why the UK Must Leave the EU

The European Union is not just a trading arrangement. It is a political project designed to take control of all the main functions of national governments. The EU controls farming and fishing, its 'harmonised' rules about everything from food-labelling to taxation already account for 70% of our laws, and it is now setting up Euro-police, systems of justice, common defence and foreign policies even though its new Constitution has not yet been agreed.

This alien system of government is bad for our economy, our self-respect and our prosperity. Yet all the old political parties remain firmly committed to the EU. They still pretend that, despite the experience of 30 years of 'negotiating', it can be shaped in Britain's interests. But the EU is a one-way street towards European government. It is undemocratic, corrupt and unreformable. The only way for Britain is UKIP's [United Kingdom Independence Party's] way: we must leave.

Until this is done, individuals and our businesses will continue to be strangled by all the ill-conceived intrusive regulation, supposedly to protect our environment, to ensure our health and safety, to uphold all our 'rights' and most recently, to protect us from terrorism.

UK Independence Party,
"UKIP Manifesto 2005," 2005.

That's working for the North East Assembly which the people of the North East roundly rejected. . . .

Because it is the EU's plan to get rid of England and to replace the House of Commons with these nine regional parliaments they are doing everything they can to destroy England as a nation.

The English Are Disappearing

You can advertise for a Scottish employee but it's racist to advertise for an English employee. Census forms and questionnaires published by the Government don't give people the chance to describe themselves as English. You can be Welsh or Chinese or Australian. But you can't be English. People have been told that they must not fly the English flag. Using traditional English measures—such as pounds and ounces—is now illegal. Though I'm delighted to say that I'm now selling some of my books by imperial weights. My book *England Our England* costs £26 a pound and my book *The Truth They Won't Tell You About The EU* is £15 a pound. I invite Trading Standards officers to arrest me if they like. The *East Kent Mercury* reported the other day that crossing the channel will soon no longer be classed as a trip abroad by the EU. The English Channel won't be the English channel. It will become a maritime space controlled by the EU. *Lloyds List* shipping newspaper says it's a sinister move that should be resisted. In 2007, the Scottish economist Adam Smith is going to appear on the English £20 note. The first time a Scot has ever appeared on a Bank of England note. Sports fans will have noticed that a growing number of England cricket, football and rugby matches are no longer shown on the BBC—despite promises that national matches would be shown on terrestrial television.

Neither the Scots nor the Welsh give a damn about all this. The Scots don't usually fly Union flags [of the United Kingdom]. They think they're going to be independent countries soon. They've been conned into thinking that their Assemblies put them just one step away from being separate countries. They want to break up the union. Sadly, they've been tricked. They're just parts of the EU and that's all that [they] will be.

There's a campaign now to have an English Parliament. It's a start—though it will never happen because neither the Government nor the EU can allow it to happen. They're solidly committed to the nine regions replacing England.

The only way that England will be saved will be for the English to insist that England leaves the EU and reverts to being an independent nation state. That's the only answer. And we can do it. If Scotland and Wales want to remain as European regions as they seem to want to do, then we'll have to let them.

The United Kingdom is doomed and beyond help.

There's just a slim, slim hope that England can be saved.

"Britain should stay in the European Union."

Great Britain Should Remain in the European Union

Richard Laming

In the following viewpoint, Richard Laming argues that the European Union (EU) is a success. Pointing to the need for countries to cooperate in a world with increased globalization, Laming cites examples of how the EU has provided solutions to common problems of member states. Consequently, Laming claims that it is in the interest of Great Britain (England, Scotland, and Wales) to remain in the EU. Richard Laming is Secretary of Federal Union, the British federalist campaigning organization, and works in public affairs for commercial interests in London and Brussels.

As you read, consider the following questions:

1. What organizations does the author identify as being similar to the European Union?

2. In what way has the European Union found solutions to environmental problems, according to Laming?

Richard Laming, "Should We Stay or Should We Go?" *Federal Union*, November 26, 2006. www.federalunion.org.uk. Reproduced by permission.

3. According to the author, in what ways is the European Union becoming more democratic?

The EU [European Union] was founded in 1957 and, at the time was called the EEC [European Economic Community] and had only 6 member states. Since that time its member states have grown in number, as more and more countries have sought to join. It has expanded to the north, to the south, to the west and, most recently, to the east. From having been a relatively small group of western European countries, it now extends to all corners of the continent.

The Need for Cooperation

It is also worth knowing that it is not alone. While in many ways it is a unique organisation—I will explain some of these ways later—there are other organisations in other parts of the world that are following the same path. There is the Association of South East Asian Nations, ASEAN, there is Mercosur [Southern Common Market] in South America, there is NAFTA [North American Free Trade Association] in North America, there is the African Union. And at global level there are international institutions like the United Nations and the Kyoto agreement for fighting climate change.

Why is it that so many countries around the world are willing to give up a little bit of their independence and share some of their sovereignty with others? Why are they choosing to cooperate?

The reason is that in many ways they are increasingly interdependent. They have more and more in common these days. This is the phenomenon called globalisation.

Faced with globalisation they need to find common solutions to common problems such as the economy and the environment.

Here in Europe, the EU has been leading the way in both these fields. Let me give some examples.

The Market Benefit for EU Members

When the EU [European Union] negotiates on behalf of its members in this organisation, it represents the world's biggest single market and as a result has more influence. Other nations are much keener to make concessions to the EU than to individual member states as they see the rewards of gaining access to the EU market as much greater than the rewards of gaining access to any individual national market.

Wayne Ives, "Arguments for the EU,"
Civitas, March 2006. www.civitas.org.uk.

The Benefit of Trade

First of all, looking at the economy, the EU has created the largest Single Market in the world. The idea behind the single market is that there should be common rules for businesses in all countries so that they can trade with each other more easily. The aim is that it should be as easy for a company based in London to trade with a company based in Paris as with one based in Birmingham [England]. There will be all kinds of cultural differences that remain, of course, but there shouldn't be any legal or bureaucratic ones.

By making it easier for companies to trade with each other, the economy grows and wealth is created as a result. The European Single Market has led to an increase in household income of about €5,700 (£3,819) over the past ten years, according to [European] Commission estimates. It has done that by measures such as abolishing the customs forms that used to have to be filled in at borders—60 million forms have been scrapped, needless bureaucracy swept away—which has in turn cut the costs of delivering goods by 15 per cent. Between 300,000 and 900,000 jobs have been created, thanks to the Single Market.

Environmental Benefits

In the environmental field, too, different countries have worked together through the EU to solve common problems. It is obvious that pollution does not stop at national borders and that shared efforts are therefore required if there is to be an effective effort to protect the environment.

For example, migratory birds are protected by the Birds Directive. There is no point in Britain trying to protect rare birds from hunting if they are going to be shot as they fly south over France or Italy. Bird protection has got to be a common effort. The REACH [Registration, Evaluation and Authorization of Chemicals] programme is a far-reaching scheme to ensure that all the chemicals used in industry are safe for humans and for the environment. It takes an organisation as big as the EU to make such a programme possible. And the EU is also pioneering a scheme for emissions trading as part of the fight against climate change. Making companies pay for the costs of their own emissions will encourage them to reduce them.

If these are some simple examples of what the European Union does, I have got to explain next why it works. Why do we need something as formal and organised as the EU rather than a simple loose coordination between different countries?

Why the EU Is a Success

I think there are three reasons why the EU works so well and has achieved things that mere cooperation never could. The Single Market was a dream for decades, but it took the European Union to make it a reality.

The first reason is that the EU is based on permanent institutions. Rather than drifting along on shifting alliances, the EU has:

- The European Commission: to represent the common European interest

- The European Parliament: directly-elected by the citizens

- The Council of Ministers: representing the national governments

These permanent institutions work together to ensure that all the different interests are considered and taken into account in making decisions.

These decisions themselves are the second reason why the EU is a success. They are not merely political decisions but have the force of law. The prime ministers of the member states are not free to ignore the decisions that they do not like: the European Court of Justice has the role of holding politicians to keep their word.

The third reason for success is the fact that the EU is becoming increasingly democratic in the way that it works and makes decisions. The directly-elected European Parliament takes a bigger role in decisions now than it did in the past; the Council of Ministers is more open in the way it reaches decisions on European law; the European Commission is confirmed in office and held to account by the European Parliament.

That alternative to the EU would be decision-making without permanent institutions, without the rule of law, and without democratic input. There would be cooperation still between countries, but without these additional features. I think that would be worse, and not better.

Britain Should Stay

Finally, against this background of what the European Union is, what it does, and why it works, I want to summarise the arguments for Britain staying in the European Union.

First of all, globalisation exists. It cannot be wished away.

Given that globalisation exists, countries have to cooperate in order to deal with it. The alternative would be to be swamped by it.

When countries cooperate, they should do so on the basis of the rule of law rather than simply relying on the word of politicians. And when those laws are made, that should be done in as democratic manner as possible.

Lastly, for Britain, the obvious place to start with international democratic cooperation are the countries with whom we have the most interests in common, namely the rest of Europe. If not the rest of Europe, there is nowhere else for Britain to go.

These are all reasons why Britain should stay in the European Union.

Periodical Bibliography

The following articles have been selected to supplement the diverse views presented in this chapter.

Hakan Altinay and Aryeh Neier
"Joining the EU: Europe Should Recognize Turkey's Progress," *International Herald Tribune*, May 7, 2004.

Paul Belien
"Eurocrats Target Poland: The Arrogance of the Elites," *Washington Times*, October 10, 2007.

Carl Bildt and Massimo D'Alemais
"It's Time for a Fresh Effort: Turkey and the EU," *International Herald Tribune*, September 2, 2007.

Daily Telegraph
"EU Is Not an Either/Or Issue," January 1, 2003.

Nikolas K. Gvosdev
"Turkey's Uphill Battle," *National Review Online*, February 19, 2004.

Leon Hadar
"Iraq and Israel in the EU: Peace through Accession?" *In the National Interest*, May 14, 2003.

Nick Larigakis
"A Macedonian Misnomer?" *Washington Times*, October 7, 2007.

Andrew Purvis
"Positive Poles," *Time*, March 26, 2007.

David Rennie
"What You Can Pick Up in Iceland," *The Spectator*, September 16, 2006.

Nicolas Sarkozy, interview
"Making France a Power for the Future, Part I," *The National Interest Online*, April 17, 2007. http://nationalinterest.org/Article.aspx?id=14044.

Benedict von Tscharner
"Switzerland's Groucho Marx Syndrome," *Europe's World*, Spring 2006.

Kjetil Wiedswang
"Happy to Be Outside the EU Club," *BBC News*, March 20, 2007.

OPPOSING
VIEWPOINTS®
SERIES

CHAPTER 3

Is the European Union Succeeding Globally?

Chapter Preface

One of the main motivators for countries to join the European Union (EU) is economic integration. This economic integration is meant to increase the economic situation of each member country as well as to help the European Union compete on a global scale with other large economic markets, such as the United States. Reviews are mixed as to whether the European Union is succeeding on either front. The situation of each member country is extremely varied and the European Union's status worldwide is debated. Nonetheless, since the European Union has many new members and continues to enlarge, it may be quite a while until the final verdict is in.

Central to the idea of economic integration and a single-market approach is freedom of access of people, capital, goods, and services. The freedom of access of people means that citizens of all EU states can study, work, and retire in any EU member state. Freedom of access of capital means that Europeans can manage and invest their money in any EU country. The freedom of access of goods means that people in the European Union may buy and sell products throughout the European Union without incurring additional costs. Finally, freedom of access of services means that services can be provided throughout the European Union without reference to the home state of the service provider.

The European Union continues to make progress toward meeting the goal of a single market. Included in this pursuit are changes to border controls allowing Europeans to travel freely, adoption of a single currency—the euro, lifting barriers to trade and developing EU-wide regulations for products, and lifting restrictions on migrant workers. Even as the European Union gets closer to the goal of a single market, there are still many barriers in the form of member country regulations and policies. Since the member countries are sovereign, each step toward economic integration must be agreed to by the member state and member states do not always see every facet of integration as in their best interest. As economic integration continues, the success of the European Union remains to be seen.

Economists, analysts, and writers debate the current state of the European Union with respect to economics and security in the following chapter, offering varying answers to the question: Is the European Union Succeeding Globally?

> "Europe has had little to offer the United
> States in strategic military terms since
> the end of the Cold War."

America Can Maintain Global Security on Its Own

Robert Kagan

In the following viewpoint, Robert Kagan claims that Americans and Europeans have very different ideas about how best to promote global security, due to their unique histories. America, he argues, is unlikely to give up its belief in the use of its power through unilateral military force. While claiming that support from Europe is preferred, Kagan believes that America will pursue its military goals with or without Europe. Robert Kagan, author of the best seller, Of Paradise and Power, *is senior associate at the Carnegie Endowment for International Peace, a private, nonprofit organization dedicated to advancing cooperation between nations.*

As you read, consider the following questions:

1. What lesson temporarily replaced the "lesson of Munich" as the dominant paradigm for American strategic thought, according to the author?

Robert Kagan, "Power and Weakness: Why the United States and Europe See the World Differently," *Policy Review*, June & July 2002. www.hoover.org/publications/policy review/3460246.html. Reproduced by permission.

2. Why does Kagan believe that the future is likely to be one of increased tension between the United States and the European Union?

3. What is the purpose, according to Kagan, of the United States engaging in some multilateralism with Europe?

Contrary to what many believe, the United States can shoulder the burden of maintaining global security without much help from Europe. The United States spends a little over 3 percent of its GDP [gross domestic product] on defense today [2002]. Were Americans to increase that to 4 percent—meaning a defense budget excess of $500 billion per year—it would still represent a smaller percentage of national wealth than Americans spent on defense throughout most of the past half-century. Even Paul Kennedy, who invented the term "imperial overstretch" in the late 1960s (when the United States was spending around 7 percent of its GDP on defense), believes the United States can sustain its current military spending levels and its current global dominance far into the future. Can the United States handle the rest of the world without much help from Europe? The answer is that it already does. The United States has maintained strategic stability in Asia with no help from Europe. In the Gulf War, European help was token; so it has been more recently in Afghanistan, where Europeans are once again "doing the dishes"; and so it would be in an invasion of Iraq to unseat Saddam [Hussein, the leader of Iraq]. Europe has had little to offer the United States in strategic military terms since the end of the Cold War—except, of course, that most valuable of strategic assets, a Europe at peace.

The United States can manage, therefore, at least in material terms. Nor can one argue that the American people are unwilling to shoulder this global burden, since they have done so for a decade already. After September 11 [2001], they seem willing to continue doing so for a long time to come. Americans apparently feel no resentment at not being able to enter a "postmodern" utopia. There is no evidence most Americans desire to. Partly because they are so powerful, they take pride in their nation's military power and their nation's special role in the world.

Americans, Unlike Europeans, Believe in Power

Americans have no experience that would lead them to embrace fully the ideals and principles that now animate Europe. Indeed, Americans derive their understanding of the world from a very different set of experiences. In the first half of the twentieth century, Americans had a flirtation with a certain kind of internationalist idealism [U.S. president Woodrow] Wilson's "war to end all wars" was followed a decade later by an American secretary of state putting his signature to a treaty outlawing war. FDR [U.S. president Franklin Delano Roosevelt] in the 1930s put his faith in non-aggression pacts and asked merely that [German leader Adolf] Hitler promise not to attack a list of countries Roosevelt presented to him. But then came Munich [where an agreement was signed by Allied and Axis nations in which Hitler vowed not to attack Czechoslovakia, but then violated the agreement] and Pearl Harbor [where Germany's ally Japan attacked the U.S. Naval base there], and then, after a fleeting moment of renewed idealism, the plunge into the Cold War. The "lesson of Munich" came to dominate American strategic thought, and although it was supplanted for a time by the "lesson of Vietnam," today it remains the dominant paradigm. While a small segment of the American elite still yearns for "global governance" and eschews military force, Americans from Madeleine Albright [former U.S. secretary of state] to Donald Rumsfeld [former secretary of defense], from Brent Scowcroft [former national security adviser] to Anthony Lake [former national security adviser], still remember Munich, figuratively if not literally. And for younger generations of Americans who do not remember Munich or Pearl Harbor, there is now September 11 [2001]. After September 11, even many American globalizers demand blood.

Americans are idealists, but they have no experience of promoting ideals successfully without power. Certainly, they have no experience of successful supranational governance; little to make them place their faith in international law and international institutions, much as they might wish to; and even less to let them travel, with the Europeans, beyond power. Americans, as good children of the Enlightenment, still believe in the perfectibility of man, and they retain hope for the perfectibility of the world. But they remain realists in the limited sense that they still believe in the necessity of power in a world that remains far from perfection. Such law as there may be to regulate international behavior, they believe, exists because a power like the United States defends it by force of arms. In other words, just as Europeans claim, Americans can still sometimes see themselves in heroic terms—as [cowboy actor] Gary Cooper at high noon. They will defend the townspeople, whether the townspeople want them to or not.

America Will Use Power, With or Without Europe

The problem lies neither in American will or capability, then, but precisely in the inherent moral tension of the current international situation. As is so often the case in human affairs, the real question is one of intangibles—of fears, passions, and beliefs. The problem is that the United States must sometimes play by the rules of a Hobbesian [self-interested] world, even though in doing so it violates European norms. It must refuse to abide by certain international conventions that may constrain its ability to fight effectively in [the European Union's external affairs director] Robert Cooper's jungle. It must support arms control, but not always for itself. It must live by a double standard. And it must sometimes act unilaterally, not out of a passion for unilateralism but, given a weak Europe that has moved beyond power, because the United States has no choice *but* to act unilaterally.

Few Europeans admit, as Cooper does implicitly, that such American behavior may redound to the greater benefit of the civilized world, that American power, even employed under a double standard, may be the best means of advancing human progress—and perhaps the only means. Instead, many Europeans today have come to consider the United States itself to be the outlaw, a rogue colossus. Europeans have complained about President [George W.] Bush's "unilateralism," but they are coming to the deeper realization that the problem is not Bush or any American president. It is systemic. And it is incurable.

Given that the United States is unlikely to reduce its power and that Europe is unlikely to increase more than marginally its own power or the will to use what power it has, the future seems certain to be one of increased transatlantic tension. The danger—if it is a danger—is that the United States and Europe will become positively estranged. Europeans will become more shrill in their attacks on the United States. The United States will become less inclined to listen, or perhaps even to care. The day could come, if it has not already, when Americans will no more heed the pronouncements of the EU than they do the pronouncements of ASEAN [Association of Southeast Asian Nations] or the Andean Pact.

To those of us who came of age in the Cold War, the strategic decoupling of Europe and the United States seems frightening. [French leader Charles] DeGaulle, when confronted by FDR's vision of a world where Europe was irrelevant, recoiled and suggested that this vision "risked endangering the Western world." If Western Europe was to be considered a "secondary matter" by the United States, would not FDR only "weaken the very cause he meant to serve—that of civilization?" Western Europe, DeGaulle insisted, was "essential to the West.

Nothing can replace the value, the power, the shining example of the ancient peoples." Typically, DeGaulle insisted this was "true of France above all." But leaving aside French *amour propre*, did not DeGaulle have a point? If Americans were to decide that Europe was no more than an irritating irrelevancy, would American society gradually become unmoored from what we now call the West? It is not a risk to be taken lightly, on either side of the Atlantic.

Support from Europe, Though Not Necessary, Is Preferable

So what is to be done? The obvious answer is that Europe should follow the course that Cooper, [British scholar Timothy Garton] Ash, [North Atlantic Treaty Organization (NATO) secretary general George] Robertson, and others recommend and build up its military capabilities, even if only marginally. There is not much ground for hope that this will happen. But, then, who knows? Maybe concern about America's overweening power really will create some energy in Europe. Perhaps the atavistic impulses that still swirl in the hearts of Germans, Britons, and Frenchmen—the memory of power, international influence, and national ambition—can still be played upon. Some Britons still remember empire; some Frenchmen still yearn for *la gloire*; some Germans still want their place in the sun. These urges are now mostly channeled into the grand European project, but they could find more traditional expression. Whether this is to be hoped for or feared is another question. It would be better still if Europeans could move beyond fear and anger at the rogue colossus and remember, again, the vital necessity of having a strong America—for the world and especially for Europe.

Americans can help. It is true that the Bush administration came into office with a chip on its shoulder. It was hostile to the new Europe—as to a lesser extent was the [Bill] Clinton administration—seeing it not so much as an ally but as an albatross. Even after September 11, when the Europeans offered their very limited military capabilities in the fight in Afghanistan, the United States resisted, fearing that European cooperation was a ruse to tie America down. The Bush administration viewed NATO's historic decision to aid the United States under Article V less as a boon than as a booby trap. An opportunity to draw Europe into common battle out in the Hobbesian world, even in a minor role, was thereby unnecessarily lost.

Americans are powerful enough that they need not fear Europeans, even when bearing gifts. Rather than viewing the United States as a Gulliver tied down by Lilliputian threads, American leaders should realize that they are hardly constrained at all, that Europe is not really capable of constraining the United States. If the United States could move past the anxiety engendered by this inaccurate sense of constraint, it could begin to show more understanding for the sensibilities of others, a little generosity of spirit. It could pay its respects to multilateralism and the rule of law and try to build some international political capital for those moments when multilateralism is impossible and unilateral action unavoidable. It could, in short, take more care to show what the founders called a "decent respect for the opinion of mankind."

These are small steps, and they will not address the deep problems that beset the transatlantic relationship today. But, after all, it is more than a cliché that the United States and Europe share a set of common Western beliefs. Their aspirations for humanity are much the same, even if their vast disparity of power has now put them in very different places. Perhaps it is not too naïvely optimistic to believe that a little common understanding could still go a long way.

> *"While the administration often points to the problems that can come from trying to mount a coalition effort, unilateral action may also lead us into dangerous strategic choices."*

America Needs the Help of the European Union for Global Security

Ronald D. Asmus and Kenneth M. Pollack

In the following viewpoint, Ronald D. Asmus and Kenneth M. Pollack argue that while the European Union and the United States differ on questions of global security, they will need to develop a joint strategy on key issues, such as bringing peace to the Middle East, if peace is to be successful. The authors acknowledge significant differences between the United States and Europe but outline several reasons why such a joint strategy is possible. Asmus is executive director of the Transatlantic Center of the German Marshall Fund of the United States in Brussels, Belgium. Pollack is a senior fellow and the director of research at the Saban Center for Middle East Policy of the Brookings Institution.

Ronald D. Asmus and Kenneth M. Pollack, "The New Transatlantic Project," *Policy Review*, October & November 2002. www.hoover.org/publications/policyreview/34592 16.html. Reproduced by permission.

As you read, consider the following questions:

1. According to the authors, what is different about the way the United States has treated Europe on the issue of the Greater Middle East, compared to the issue of Moscow during the Cold War?

2. What do the authors fear would result from the U.S. decision to pursue a unilateral, largely military, approach with the Greater Middle East without involvement from Europe?

3. What three conditions did Europe have for supporting the United States in the war in Iraq, according to the authors?

Although September 11 [2001] initially produced a tremendous outpouring of solidarity across the Atlantic, the mood has since soured into one of the ugliest U.S.-European spats in recent memory. It has become fashionable on both sides to argue that the differences today [2002] are deeper than ever, and that the values and interests that held this relationship together may be in danger of fraying or even breaking. Euro-trashing is as much in vogue in some right-wing circles in Washington as America-bashing is in left-wing circles in Europe.

Disputes Between Europe and the United States

Current transatlantic differences are real. But it is also important to look beyond the current intellectual fads and see what underlies them—and what doesn't. U.S.-European differences fall into two categories. The first are those disputes that arise from the fact that our societies are more integrated than any two parts of the planet. Clashes over the environment, child custody, the death penalty, and genetically modified food are important and make for great headlines. But they are not strategic in nature. The fact that we are debating them so intensely is a sign of how closely integrated our societies have become. They are the problems of success, not failure. Such differences were far greater in 1949. They did not prevent us from creating a strategic alliance then. They should not prevent us from working together on a new strategic agenda today.

But there is also a second category of differences. These disputes revolve around how the U.S. and Europe view the outside world, assess threats, and seek to meet them. They are rooted not only in our respective interests but are shaped by our size, historical experiences, strategic culture, and the asymmetry in power and responsibility that both sides of the Atlantic bring to the table. Such differences directly affect our ability, or lack thereof, to cooperate on questions of war and peace. They can become strategic in nature. The central question in the transatlantic relationship today is whether the U.S. and Europe can still harmonize these differences and coalesce around a new strategic purpose and paradigm to guide future cooperation across the Atlantic.

At first glance there are few issues or places where the gap across the Atlantic would appear to be greater than the thorny strategic issues of bringing peace to the Greater Middle East. Making this challenge the centerpiece of transatlantic cooperation is akin to mission impossible, critics will suggest. Without underestimating or downplaying these differences, several caveats are nevertheless needed to put them into perspective.

Europe and the United States Have Much in Common

First, until the present, neither the U.S. nor Europe felt a compelling strategic need to have a common strategy on these issues. Neither side of the Atlantic has been willing to make the political commitment to develop one. When it came to dealing with Moscow during the Cold War, both sides of the At-

Europe Has Its Own Unique Power

Why is it that Americans do not understand the power of the European Union [EU]? Is it because they are simply not well informed by reports from Brussels [Belgium, headquarters of the EU executive arm] and other European capitals? Or is it because, as citizens of the world's last truly sovereign nation-state, Americans—and especially American conservatives—find it difficult to acknowledge the contribution of a transnational organization based on supranational law? It's as if they can conceive of power only in the old-fashioned terms of a classical nation-state.

Timothy Garton Ash, New York Times, *December 17, 2004.*

lantic relied on each other's counsel, cooperation, and commitment to forge a common approach. But this has rarely been the case in the Greater Middle East. The U.S. has often preferred to keep Europe on the sidelines, and key European countries had their own reasons to pursue a go-it-alone approach. Both sides no longer have that luxury in the wake of September 11.

Second, U.S.-European differences on the key issues in the Greater Middle East, while often bitter, are largely tactical and not strategic in nature. They relate not to ends but to the means by which to reach them. Americans and Europeans do not disagree over Israel's right to exist or the need for a Palestinian state and a peace settlement—and, at the end of the day, Europe is likely to support almost any settlement to the Arab-Israeli conflict that the U.S. can bring about. Nor does Europe oppose toppling Saddam Hussein, although it has grave doubts about how the [George W.] Bush administration might go about doing so and what Washington's policy is for the day after. [A U.S.-led invasion of Iraq in March 2003 led to the removal of Hussein and the war in Iraq.] Yet these differences are not necessarily deeper than the issues that divided us during the Cold War over how best to deal with Moscow.

Third, past U.S.-European differences did not prevent the West from winning the Cold War. The alliance won not because we agreed on everything all the time but because there was a commitment to face the challenge together, to share risks and responsibilities, and to work within a common framework to iron out differences. U.S.-European consultations were not always a hindrance but often led to better policy as many a foolish American or European idea got shot down in the process. Nor did the West prevail simply because of U.S. military power. Americans and Europeans still debate whether [U.S. president] Ronald Reagan's arms buildup or [German chancellor] Willy Brandt's *Ostpolitik* was more important in bringing communism to its knees. Ultimately, it was the one-two punch of soft and hard power provided by Europe and America that helped undermine and eventually topple communism.

All of this suggests that bringing the U.S. and Europe together around such a new and ambitious strategic agenda, while certainly difficult, is doable. The fundamental problem bedeviling the transatlantic relationship today is the lack of a common strategic purpose and a shared commitment on both sides of the Atlantic that would generate the will to harmonize divergent views and create a joint strategy.

A Joint Strategy Will Benefit Both

Achieving such a new consensus would have clear-cut strategic benefits for both sides. A common U.S.-European front would leave our adversaries with less room for maneuver. Working together would give Washington a degree of political acceptance and international legitimacy the U.S. cannot acquire on its own. While the U.S. will be a dominant partner in many areas, there are other areas where Europe is not only more willing, but also potentially more able, to achieve the kinds of results we need.

A common approach could also give the U.S. more and better strategic options. If the U.S. chooses to go it alone, our actions will be circumscribed by what we can do on our own. It could lead us to opt for a more limited, largely military approach—but also one that would fail to get at the root causes of the problem and would therefore be less likely to succeed. While the administration often points to the problems that can come from trying to mount a coalition effort, unilateral action may also lead us into dangerous strategic choices.

As strong as the United States is today, we are deluding ourselves if we think we can meet this strategic challenge by ourselves. Afghanistan is a sober reminder in this regard. While the U.S. did the lion's share of fighting to defeat the Taliban [government of Afghanistan], we soon discovered that our dependence on European assistance was considerable. Today there are more European forces on the ground than American. When it comes to the arduous effort of rebuilding Afghanistan, our policy is dependent on the close cooperation and support of our European and other allies.

The same is likely to be true when it comes to the other pieces of the Greater Middle Eastern puzzle. A sustainable peace settlement of the Arab-Israeli conflict will require close U.S.-European support and cooperation. Some Americans may prefer that the U.S. fight Saddam Hussein on its own, but a common U.S.-European front would make the job much easier. And when it comes to the thorny question of securing and rebuilding Iraq after Saddam is gone, we will be even more dependent on the assistance and, support of our European allies. The list is almost endless.

The U.S. Should Seek Cooperation with Europe

Is Europe up to this challenge? Our allies have not yet had their own "Pearl Harbor," [i.e., a grave event leading into war] forcing them to fundamentally rethink their national priorities the way Americans have since September 11, 2001. One can only hope that Europe will learn from America's mistakes. It may take a major terrorist attack in Europe to provide that jolt—just as it did here. But this does not mean that European elite and public attitudes have not shifted at all. European governments have already gone farther than many expected in providing intelligence support, cooperating on law enforcement issues, and working together on the financial and economic aspects of the war on terrorism. While Europe has fallen behind the United States, collectively they remain the second most powerful set of militaries in the world. With modest investments in key areas, our allies can take on an even greater share of the burden in the future.

Europeans are also feeling increasingly vulnerable. In terms of public support, a recent study conducted by the Chicago Council on Foreign Relations and the German Marshall Fund, as well as the US government's own public opinion polls, suggest that potential majority support exists in many key European states for the use of force to rid Saddam of his weapons of mass destruction. In spite of all the press coverage over European nervousness regarding U.S. policy on Iraq, many allies in private are signaling that they are prepared, in principle, to go to war in Iraq as long as they are convinced that it will be done right—that Washington will obtain UN [United Nations] authorization, has a credible strategy for ensuring that such a war does not destabilize the region, and is committed to working with Europe to rebuild Iraq after Saddam is gone.

Ultimately, Europeans, precisely because they share our values, are likely to be the most dependable allies we have. Indeed, for the more ambitious strategy this article lays out, their cooperation is indispensable. And in fact, the more ambitious agenda called for here is more likely to attract European support than the [George W.] Bush administration's current approach.

This does not mean that Europe will give the U.S. a blank check. As they did during the Cold War Europeans will ask realistic and, at times, pointed questions. We will have to work to gain their support. They are looking for a common strategic framework and a say commensurate with the risks they assume and the resources they devote. That is normal among friends and allies—and we would behave no differently if roles were reversed. We should listen to their questions and criticism. If we can't answer them, maybe we need to take a second look at our own strategy. If we are convinced that we need to go ahead in any case and despite their doubts, we can always do so.

> *"The average European only has about two-thirds the income of the average American."*

The Economy of the European Union Is Not Doing Well

Richard W. Rahn

In the following viewpoint, Richard W. Rahn argues that the European Union (EU) member countries disagree about what kind of economy the EU should model. As a result of this, Rahn claims that the EU is not doing as well economically as the United States. Rahn points to various reasons for the poor European economy, including the reluctance in some countries to employ workers from new EU member nations, the split on trade policy, and the move toward higher taxes in some nations. Rahn is director general of the Center for Global Economic Growth and an economic columnist.

As you read, consider the following questions:

1. According to the author, why does the United States have a large interest in the EU economy?

Richard W. Rahn, "Europe Vs. Europe," *The Washington Times*, October 31, 2005, p. A19. Copyright © 2005 News World Communications, Inc. Reproduced by permission.

2. What is the difference between EU countries that have allowed workers from the new Eastern European EU members and those EU countries that have not allowed such workers, according to Rahn?

3. According to the author, what approach toward taxes is adopted among EU countries that have high growth?

Is it a sensible idea to move the site of government every three weeks? This is precisely what the European Union [EU] does every month, since much of its government moves back and forth—with great wagon trains of trucks carrying government papers (and the luggage of the European parliamentarians)—between this picturesque city [Strasbourg, France] in the Rhine Valley and Brussels, Belgium.

Not only have the Europeans been unable to agree on having one capital city for the EU, but they are split on almost every major issue, making the political differences between the major parties in the U.S. seem almost inconsequential. The fundamental disagreement is to what extent Europe should move away from the "social market economy" model that has left France, Germany and Italy in economic stagnation and towards a more classic market economy such as that practiced in the U.S.

The EU Economy and the U.S. Economy

The EU has roughly the same GDP [gross domestic product] as the U.S.—each producing almost 30 percent of the world's GDP. But the EU has a third again as many people as the U.S., and hence the average European only has about two-thirds the income of the average American. The 25 nation EU [as of 2005], taken as whole, is America's biggest trading and investment partner, far outstripping China or Japan. Thus Americans and Europeans have an enormous interest in each others' economic well-being, because an economic "cold" on one side of the Atlantic will almost always be "caught" on the other side.

What Europe Needs Economically

What the bulk of the EU [European Union] desperately needs is economic growth. Instead of creating hundreds more jobs for Eurocrats, Euro-diplomats, and Euro-politicians with global pretensions, it should be creating millions of real jobs for the growing army of unemployed that truly threatens economic vitality and political stability.

That means real economic reform, including deregulation and more flexible labor markets. There may not be much the United States can do directly to assist in that process except offer encouragement.

Gerard Baker, The Weekly Standard, June 20, 2005.

Europe has been growing at roughly half the rate of the U.S. for the last two decades, which is not good for Europe or America. However, within Europe, there are considerable disparities in growth rates between countries. Those in the center—France, Germany and Italy—have barely grown, while those on the edges—Ireland, Spain, Britain and the new EU member transition countries in Central and Eastern Europe—have been for the most part doing very well. These growth disparities are causing increased tension among the 25 EU member states, and may even result in the currently strong Euro—which is the common currency of 12 European countries—becoming dysfunctional.

Reasons for the Poor EU Economy

The "Polish plumber" has become the metaphor for the philosophical split in Europe. France has all but closed its doors to allowing workers from the new Eastern European EU members to get work permits, on the misguided notion that these highly motivated people will take jobs from French workers.

Britain, Ireland, Sweden and others have taken the opposite tack and welcomed the new workers from Poland, Lithuania, Slovakia and so on, because they understand that more people working productively create more wealth and hence more jobs. The result is Britain has an unemployment rate of only 4.7 percent, even though it has absorbed more than 200,000 new workers from Eastern Europe during the last year, while France and Germany have more than 10 percent of their workforce unemployed, despite (or actually because of) their restrictive work practice.

Europe is also split on trade policy. While many of the European countries understand that freer trade leads to lower prices and a higher standard of living, some countries, again notably France, are resisting. This past week [October 2005] the French vetoed reducing farm subsidies, despite offers from the U.S. and some European countries to do so on a multilateral basis. This was highly hypocritical, given their calls for others, particularly the U.S., to give more foreign aid from coerced taxpayers. The best foreign aid would be to give African and other farmers from low income countries the opportunity to sell their goods in the rich states—but the French, again, said "Non."

The high growth countries of Europe understand that high taxes, particularly on capital and labor, kill incentives and lead to economic stagnation. France, Germany and some others, fearing productive tax competition, have pushed for "tax harmonization," which is nothing more than a code word for a high tax cartel. The outcome of these tax and regulation struggles within Europe will determine whether Europe as a whole remains one of the two great economic powers on the globe, or slowly slips behind China and the other Asian countries.

[In late October 2005] . . . in a chateau near Strasbourg, a small group of U.S. and European business leaders had a two-day meeting with representatives of several European free market activist groups. The goal of the meeting was to share ideas on how to encourage European political leaders to undertake more pro-growth economic policies so modern day Europe does not follow the fate of the Roman Empire. Looking at Germany, France and Italy, the pro-growth leaders found plenty to be pessimistic about. But they also understood that in times of crisis real change for the better can take place, which is why they are willing to spend time and money to help convince millions of Europeans to save themselves.

> *"Over the last 30 years, productivity growth has been much higher in Europe than in the United States."*

The Economy of the European Union Is Doing Well

Olivier J. Blanchard

In the following viewpoint, Olivier J. Blanchard argues that the view of the European Union as economically challenged in comparison to the United States is flawed. Blanchard challenges the way certain data is interpreted to support the view of the "euro-pessimists" and offers his own view that portrays Europe as economically strong. Blanchard is professor of economics at Massachusetts Institute of Technology (MIT) and is the author of numerous articles and books on the economy of Europe.

As you read, consider the following questions:

1. According to Blanchard, what do critics identify as the problem with Europe's economy that worked well for postwar Europe, but does not work now?

2. The author claims the pessimistic view cites what two facts in support of the claim that Europe is economically failing?

Olivier J. Blanchard, "Is Europe Falling Behind?" *The Globalist*, June 8, 2004. http://theglobalist.com. Reproduced by permission of the author.

3. In what two ways have countries of the European Union chosen to allocate gains in productivity, according to Blanchard?

After three years of near stagnation, the mood in Europe is definitely gloomy.

The two economic books on the bestseller list in France in 2003 are called *La France qui Tombe* (*The Fall of France*) and *Le Desarroi Français* (*The French Disarray*).

Both books offer a pessimistic vision of France and its economic future, a future in which—unless dramatic reforms are implemented—France will steadily lose ground against its competitors.

France is not alone. All over Europe, governments are trying to put on a good face. But their boasts—such as the goal adopted at the EU [European Union] Lisbon conference in March 2000 to make the European Union "the world's most dynamic and competitive economy within ten years"—are seen largely as empty rhetoric, if not pathetic.

A Pessimistic Assessment

The most articulate diagnoses of where Europe stands today argue that—like Stalinist growth [communism] in another time and place—the European model worked well for post-war Europe, but is no longer fit for these times.

For much of the post-war period, the argument goes, European growth was based on the notion of "catch-up growth," based primarily on imitation rather than innovation. For such growth, large European firms—protected in both goods and financial markets—could do a good job.

They could do much of the R&D [research and development] in-house. They could develop comfortable long-term relations with suppliers of funds. Best of all, they could offer long-term relationships and job security to their workers.

The ample rents generated in the European goods markets could be shared between firms and workers, and could always be counted on to help finance the welfare state.

Now that European growth must increasingly be based on innovation, now that firms cannot be insulated from foreign competition, the European model has become dysfunctional, this argument concludes.

As a result, relations between firms and suppliers of funds, between firms and their workers, must all be redefined. This requires nothing short of a complete transformation of Europe's pattern of economic and social relations.

So far, the argument concludes, Europe has not risen to the challenge. Instead, it seems increasingly petrified, unable to engage in fundamental reforms. This is why the future is bleak.

I have a more optimistic assessment.

Why the Pessimists Are Wrong

Two facts are often cited by euro-pessimists: GDP [gross domestic product] per person in the European Union, measured at purchasing power parity (PPP) prices, stands at 70% of the U.S. level of GDP per person. Not only that, but this ratio is the same as it was 30 years ago.

These facts are correct. They suggest a Europe stuck at a substantially lower standard of living than the United States— and unable to catch up. However, this interpretation would be misleading.

Things are not so bad. Over the last 30 years, productivity growth has been much higher in Europe than in the United States. And productivity levels are roughly similar today in the EU and in the United States.

The main difference is that Europe has used some of the increase in productivity to increase leisure rather than income—while the United States has done the opposite.

Europe Is Economically Strong

The European Union [EU] is now the largest internal single market as well as the largest trader of goods in the world. The EU is also the world's largest trader in services. In the year 2000, the EU accounted for 590.8 billion euros, or 24 percent of the total world trade in services, compared to the U.S., who ranked second with 550.9 billion euros and a share of 22 percent. Japan was a distant third, with 201.6 billion and an 8 percent share of the global market. Moreover, unlike the United States, which runs on a trade deficit and imports more than it exports, the EU exports more than it imports.

The European Union's Gross Domestic Product [GDP] of $10.5 trillion in 2003 already exceeds the United States' $10.4 trillion GDP and . . . even this figure masks additional economic strengths relative to America that are not accounted for in the GDP numbers. The bottom line is that the EU's GDP already comprises nearly 30 percent of the GDP of the world, making the European Union a formidable competitor to America in the global economy. (The EU's GDP is nearly 6.5 times larger than China's.)

Jeremy Rifkin, The European Dream, *2004.*

The stability of the U.S.-EU gap in relative income on a per capita basis comes from the decline in hours worked. To be specific, in the United States, over the period 1970 to 2000, GDP per hour increased by 38%. Hours worked per person also increased, by 26%. Thus, GDP per person increased by 64%.

In France, over the same period, GDP per hour increased by 83%. But hours worked per person decreased by 23%—so GDP per capita only increased by 60%.

The EU Has Allocated Gains Differently than the U.S.

Viewed in that light, the performance of France—and of the European Union in general—does not look so bad. The EU had a much higher productivity growth rate than the United States. And the EU countries chose to allocate part of those gains to increased income—and part to increased leisure.

True, unemployment has increased and is too high. But most of the decrease in hours worked per capita reflects a decrease in hours worked per worker—rather than higher unemployment or lower participation.

This choice, however, does not suggest that a deep and wide-ranging reform process is not taking place in Europe. As a matter of fact, this process is driven by reforms in financial and product markets. Reforms in those markets are, in turn, increasing pressure for reform in the European labor market as well.

Significant reform in the European labor market will eventually take place, but it could not happen overnight—and not without political tensions. These tensions have dominated and will continue to dominate the news. But they are a symptom of change—not a reflection of immobility.

| *"Aggregate hours worked are much lower*
in Europe than in the U.S."

Europe's Employment Practices Hurt the European Union Economy

Bruce Bartlett

In the following viewpoint, Bruce Bartlett argues that the economy of the European Union is lagging because Europeans do not work as much as Americans. As a result, Bartlett claims, Europeans have a lower standard of living. Bartlett hypothesizes that the reason Europeans do not work as much as Americans is because of high income taxes paid in Europe. Bruce Bartlett is an economist and writer, and he formerly served as deputy assistant secretary for economic policy at the U.S. Treasury Department.

As you read, consider the following questions:

1. According to Bartlett, how does the per capita gross domestic product (GDP) of the major countries of Europe compare to that of the United States?

2. How do Europeans and Americans differ with respect to number of paid days off, according to the author?

3. Why does the author believe that high taxes explain why Europeans take more leisure time than Americans?

Europeans are frustrated. They have been behind the United States economically for years and thought this was due to lack of economic integration. So they created the European Union, with a common currency and virtually free mobility of goods, capital, and labor throughout the continent. Yet Europe continues to lag.

The GDP per Person in the EU

A new report from the Bureau of Labor Statistics shows the U.S. with real gross domestic product [GDP] per person in 2003 of $34,960 (in 1999 dollars). This is well above every European country. The most productive European country, Norway, has a per capita GDP of just $30,882 (converted using purchasing power parity exchange rates). The major countries of Europe are even further behind: United Kingdom ($26,039), France ($25,578), Italy ($24,894), and Germany ($24,813).

In other words, Europeans produce no more per year than Americans did 20 years ago. And they are not catching up. According to the Bank for International Settlements in Switzerland, the productivity gap between the U.S. and Europe is actually widening. In the Euro area as a whole, workers were 86 percent as productive as American workers in 1995. In 2003, this fell to 84 percent.

As a consequence, living standards are much lower in Europe than most Americans imagine. This fact is highlighted in a new study by the Swedish think tank Timbro. For example, it notes that the average poor family here [in the United States] has 25 percent more living space than the average European. Looking at all American households, we have about twice as much space: 1,875 square feet here versus 976.5 square feet in

Europe. On average, Europeans only live about as well as those in the poorest American state, Mississippi.

Europeans Do Not Work as Much as Americans

Where Europeans are better off, perhaps, is in terms of leisure—they have a lot of it. According to the Union Bank of Switzerland, the typical European has two to three times as many paid days off per year as Americans. And according to Eurostat, Europeans don't put in much of a workday, either. According to the report, the typical European only does a bit more than 5 hours of gainful work per day, with Norwegians at the low end at 4 hours, 56 minutes per day, and (surprisingly) the French at the high end at 5 hours, 44 minutes per day.

One reason for the short workday is that Europeans seem to get sick a lot more than Americans. According to a July 25 [2004] report in the *New York Times*, on an average day 25 percent of Norway's workers call in sick. A 2002 study in Sweden found that the average worker there took more than 30 sick days per year. Makes you wonder just how good their health-care systems really are.

As a consequence, aggregate hours worked are much lower in Europe than in the U.S. According to a new report from the Organization for Economic Cooperation and Development [OECD] in Paris, last year the average American worked 1,792 hours. By contrast, the average Frenchman worked just 1,453 hours and the average German worked only 1,446 hours. Twenty-five years ago, annual hours worked in Europe were much closer to those here.

High Taxes Are to Blame

The OECD blames the unwillingness of Europeans to work as the principal reason for the lower output per worker and their lower standard of living compared with Americans. "Research

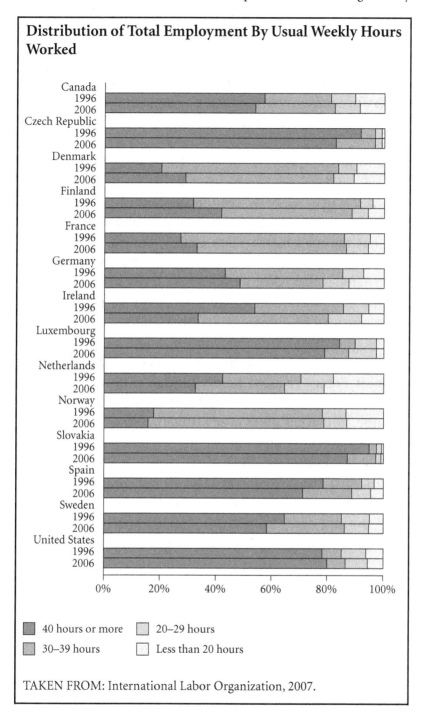

Distribution of Total Employment By Usual Weekly Hours Worked

TAKEN FROM: International Labor Organization, 2007.

has clearly established a remarkable fact: namely, that the sizable U.S. advantage in real GDP per capita . . . is largely due to differences in total hours worked per capita," the report states. It urges European governments to reform their labor policies to increase work hours, a recommendation seconded in a recent report from the International Monetary Fund [IMF].

Unfortunately, neither the OECD nor the IMF has any real explanation for why Europeans take so much leisure time. However, a new study by economist Edward Prescott of the Federal Reserve Bank of Minneapolis provides the answer. He says that Europe's higher taxes explain almost all the difference in labor-force participation rates between Europe and here. He notes that when European tax levels were comparable to those here, work hours were similar. But as Europe's taxes have risen, workers responded by working less.

Consequently, tax cuts in Europe would raise labor supplies, increase output, and raise the standard of living. For example, if France reduced its tax burden from 60 percent of GDP to 40 percent, the average Frenchman would be able to consume 19 percent more over his lifetime than he does now. This is a very large impact.

In short, Europeans don't work because it just doesn't pay to work after the government takes its cut. And because welfare benefits are so high, the cost of not working is low. Thus, when workers compare what they make after-tax with what they can make by doing nothing, the gap is very small.

> *"The threat to Europe right now is the violence of the rhetoric against the model, the bizarre gloom and doom when it is actually doing well."*

Europe's Employment Practices Do Not Hurt the European Union Economy

Thomas Geoghegan

In the following viewpoint, Thomas Geoghegan argues that despite the alarmist talk, Europe's economy is doing very well—better in many ways than that of the United States. Geoghegan claims that Europe has accomplished the remarkable by raising the standard of living while keeping its industrial base intact. Rather than cave to the interests of those that want to make Europe more like America, Geoghegan argues that Europe ought to keep the current model. Geoghegan is a labor lawyer and writer.

As you read, consider the following questions:

1. According to Geoghegan, what factor in calculating the standard of living in Europe might suggest the standard of living is going up faster in the European Union than in the United States?

2. What reason does the author give to explain the ruined industrial base of the United States?

3. What country has the highest labor costs while being the world's biggest exporter, according to Geoghegan?

The no vote on the EU [European Union] Constitution by the French, then the Dutch. The fall, or seeming fall, of the [Gerhard] Schröder government in Germany. Is Europe melting down? My friend V in Berlin says, "Relax—it's just democracy." Yet there is alarmist talk now that the EU might break up, or the euro be withdrawn.

Europe Is Doing Better than the United States

To hear the violent rhetoric from the business elites in Frankfurt and London, Europe's shambles. In fact, things are pretty nice. Yes, French unemployment is at a very distressing 10 percent. But in Europe, while it can be much harder to get a job, it is much harder to lose one, too. In a two-year period, your chance of being jobless, laid off, is probably greater in America than it would be in France, and certainly greater than in many European countries. We may have lower unemployment at any given point, but it is a kind of "rolling" unemployment, shorter but still heart-stopping, that over time will affect a larger proportion of us. Would French workers want "lower" US-style unemployment, which means a greater likelihood of layoffs, firings, drop-offs into poverty for a half-year at a time every other year? I think not.

Indeed, except for Germany (dragged down by the cost of unification), Europe or the "euro-zone" part of it has been doing at least as well as the United States in the past ten years. This is among the stunning findings of a January 2004 Goldman Sachs study, *Euroland's Secret Success Story*. As set out in the study, it's true of productivity growth—a bit under 2 percent a year in both, if adjusted for the business cycle. It's true for growth in GDP [gross domestic product] per capita (2.1 percent). And, yes, it's true even for investors: In Europe you get the same return on capital. It's true despite Europe's higher nominal unemployment and shorter workweek. Indeed, if one could put a cash value on this extra leisure, one could argue the standard of living is going up *faster* there.

But that understates the case for Europe. While too few of us in America experience any rising GDP per capita in our own lives, the egalitarian Europeans do. Outside Britain, their people at the top are not doing nearly as well as ours. That may explain the violence of their rhetoric. In France the gap between "top" and "bottom" is slightly decreasing. It might have continued to do so in Germany, too, but for the skewing of all measures by East Germany. Yes, German unions have had to keep wages down of late. But that's at least in part because in the early 1990s they pushed them up too high, even by my left-of-center standards. In total job growth, too, Europe's been doing better than the United States.

Some economists even argue America overstates its productivity growth and GDP per capita. For example, Europe doesn't get our unfair productivity boost from people working off the clock. Or the GDP growth from building far more prisons. It's plausible that in the past ten years most of Europe has done better than the United States—even as Europeans keep working fewer hours.

Europe Should Keep the Current Model

Still, the business elites say the European model has to go. In a flat world, as [economics columnist] Thomas Friedman proclaims, it seems obvious that high-wage Europeans will have to make a bonfire of their cushy way of life if they want to keep their precious industrial base.

There's one problem with using the US and UK [United Kingdom] models for saving Europe's industrial base: Both have wrecked their industrial bases. Some, or a labor lawyer

High Wages and Benefits Are Good for Europe

Critics routinely claim that high European wages and social-welfare benefits stall job creation, and that Europeans "resist reform." In fact, there's no evidence for this. If it were so, how then could Europe have enjoyed higher economic growth than America for the bulk of the postwar era? Despite nearly 50 percent tax rates and cradle-to-grave welfare benefits. Northern European social democracies like Denmark, Sweden and Finland grab half of the top slots in the World Economic Forum's ranking of the world's most competitive economies. "Nordic social democracy remains robust," says Anthony Giddens, former head of the London School of Economics—"not because it has resisted reform, but because it embraced it."

Insofar as per capita European growth lags the United States, it is not because Europeans are uncompetitive. Take Germany, with a larger trade surplus than China's and a growing share of world trade. Output per hour worked is higher in France than in the United States. *Daily* U.S. productivity is higher than in Europe only because employed Europeans choose to work fewer hours than Americans, in exchange for less pay. Remember those six to eight weeks of vacation every European is assured? Most Americans say they would make the same trade-off—if only their employers would permit it.

Andrew Moravcsik, Newsweek International,
March 26, 2007.

like me, would argue that we wrecked ours not because our labor costs were too high but because they were too low. In the low-cost United States a firm can shut down and pay workers next to nothing—and the investors can open up a

Wal-Mart. By contrast, in high-cost Europe, with expensive "closing plans" and labor vetoes in Germany and France, it is much harder than in the low-cost United States for a firm to go out of its industrial business altogether.

Over and over I hear intelligent people in America ohh and ahh over the China miracle, and China's export prowess. "Oh, China is what's happening." "China changes everything." I don't mean to scoff, but China is simply doing what others—Japan, for example—have done before. It's ordinary catch-up. But Europe, and in particular Germany, is doing something truly new. Its highly developed countries have somehow kept their industrial base.

Last year, according to the WTO [World Trade Organization], German export goods had a value of more than $915 billion. China's had a value of about $593 billion. In a so-called flat world, it turns out that the country with the world's highest labor cost is the world's champion exporter. And in France et al., and EU is even further ahead—last year, it had export goods of more than $1.5 trillion. What's more, the endless dire talk in Germany about losing it all to Eastern Europe has turned out to be wildly overstated. It's now 2005, and the recent data show that far from investing more in Eastern Europe, Germany of late has been slightly disinvesting. Of course, there is more outsourcing to Eastern Europe, but the bottom line is that Germany's overall trade surplus is growing. US and other companies have passed over Germany and put money into Eastern Europe, and labor cost is one reason, but an equal and bigger reason is simply that there is a huge untapped market in Eastern Europe, while Western Europe is relatively sated. Yet Germans bemoan it, and neoliberals have been brilliant at rattling German self-confidence over, well, not much.

The European miracle is often said to be the one that took place in the 1950s, right after World War II. But that was catch-up, too. The real European miracle is the one that has happened in the past ten years: Europe (i.e., France and Germany) has engaged in a restructuring of its manufacturing—successfully. The threat to Europe right now is the violence of the rhetoric against the model, the bizarre gloom and doom when it is actually doing well. The nerve-racking thing about Europe at the moment is the possibility that ordinary Europeans will lose their nerve and just cave in to their American-wannabe elites.

*"Airbus was born, and continues to ex-
ist, as a creature of EU subsidies."*

Airbus and Other
European Companies Get
Unfair Advantages

Investor's Business Daily

In the following viewpoint, the editors of Investor's Business
Daily *argue that the European company Airbus is operating un-
fairly by using government subsidies to succeed. Such subsidies,
the authors argue, put U.S. companies, like Boeing, at a disad-
vantage and are a threat to free trade. The authors suggest the
European Union [EU] act quickly to correct this problem so that
American companies do not suffer and begin to seek their own
protectionist measures from the U.S. government. The* Investor's
Business Daily *is a newspaper covering investment news.*

As you read, consider the following questions:

1. According to the authors, what was Airbus's response to
   Boeing's plans for the 787?

Investor's Business Daily, "The EU's Trade Charade," June 1, 2005, p. A13. www.ib
deditorials.com. Copyright © Investor's Business Daily, Inc. 2000-2008. All right re-
served. Reproduced by permission.

2. What is the difference in growth of imports since 1997 between the United States and the European Union, according to *Investor's Business Daily*?

3. What do the authors claim that the EU economy values, in contrast to the postwar world economy values of free trade and globalization?

Tired of endless negotiations, the U.S. late Monday [May 30, 2005] announced it will ask the World Trade Organization to sanction the 25-nation EU [European Union] for its illegal subsidies to Airbus.

Subsidies to Airbus Are Unfair

And who can argue America doesn't have a good case? Airbus was born, and continues to exist, as a creature of EU subsidies. Its successes are the result of massive government aid—and extensive arm-twisting of potential foreign buyers by EU bureaucrats. The subsidies have gone on for years, amounting to billions of dollars in unfair help. But what finally pushed the U.S. over the edge was Airbus' request for $1.7 billion in new EU aid. You see, Boeing has a new jet, the 787, and it looks like a winner. So cash-strapped Airbus wants to build a new plane too.

This is unfair trade, plain and simple, and the EU doesn't really deny it. It only counters that Boeing has received $23 billion in "hidden subsidies" over the years in the form of U.S. government and military contracts. (Of course, by such absurd logic, no private company anywhere would be able to contract with any government.)

So, in response to the U.S. announcement, the EU said it would file a counter-complaint against Boeing. In doing so, however, it all but admitted its action was little more than a nuisance suit.

Subsidies to Airbus

Airbus S.A.S. ("Airbus") was established in 1970 as a European consortium of French, German, and later, Spanish and U.K. [United Kingdom] companies. In 2001, Airbus formally became a single integrated company. The European Aeronautic Defence and Space Company ("EADS") and BAE SYSTEMS of the U.K. transferred all of their Airbus-related assets to the newly incorporated company and became 80 percent and 20 percent, respectively, owners of the company. The operating results of Airbus are fully consolidated in the EADS balance sheet.

Over its 35 year history, Airbus has benefited from massive amounts of EU member state and EU subsidies that have enabled the company to create a full product line of aircraft and gain a 50 percent share of large commercial aircraft ("LCA") sales and a 60 percent share of the global order book. Every major Airbus aircraft model was financed, in whole or in part, with EU government subsidies taking the form of "launch aid"—financing with no or low rates of interest, and repayment tied to sales of the aircraft. If the sales of a particular model are less than expected, Airbus does not have to repay the remainder of the financing. EU governments have forgiven Airbus debt; provided equity infusions; provided dedicated infrastructure support; and provided substantial amounts or research and development funds for civil aircraft projects.

Office of the United States Trade Representative (USTR),
October 6, 2004.

"The WTO [World Trade Organization] has better things to do than referee this grudge fight between Airbus and Boeing," said EU Trade Commissioner Peter Mandelson. We respectfully disagree.

There's more at stake in the outcome of this debate than just these two companies. This is also about the future of free trade—and whether U.S. companies, faced with a growing backlash in the EU and elsewhere, can ever get a fair shake in foreign markets. We'd be foolish to sit by and let our champions—like planemaker Boeing—be targeted by foreign governments for anti-competitive action. To do so risks billions in trade and jobs.

A trade war could prove disastrous—for the U.S., yes, but even more so for the EU. The U.S. and EU this year [2005] will have nearly $472 billion in total trade, most of it coming in the form of imports to the U.S. from Europe. Since 1997, U.S. imports from the EU have grown at an average 7.9% a year. U.S. sales to Europe, meanwhile, haven't done so well—growing at a pathetic 3.3%.

EU Trade Surplus Is a Sign of Weakness

With our trade gap widening and the EU intent on attacking U.S. companies that do well, it won't be long before America's own home-grown protectionists start pressuring Washington to erect barriers of its own. This would be a huge mistake. The time for the EU to act is now. Its economic leaders—if that's not too generous a term—have saddled the continent with welfare and tax burdens that have left both its workers and its companies uncompetitive. That's Europe's dirty secret: Its soaring trade surplus with the U.S. is due to its no-growth economy, not protectionism. It's a sign of weakness, not strength.

Yet, the EU's bureaucrats act as if protectionism will save Europe. It won't.

That makes the battle for trade fairness—and for broad economic reforms in Europe's welfare state—even more crucial.

As we said, this is not just about Boeing. It's about other companies, too. Like Microsoft: It's undergoing a full-body

cavity search by EU officials intent on fining the software gi-
ant because it has crushed all of its European competitors.

And it's about Procter & Gamble and Gillette, whose epic
$57 billion merger could be hindered by an EU investigation
launched Tuesday [May 31, 2005]. These companies are American, not European.

Enough is enough. In economic circles it is widely accepted that the postwar world economy has been built on free
trade and globalization. Yet, the road the EU seems to be trav-
eling is toward closed markets and protectionism. The EU
worries that if it doesn't attack America's best, it'll be left in
the dust. Well, it's right. Europe is losing that fight. The correct response, however, isn't more protectionism and government subsidies. It's more competition and private-sector dy-
namism—two things that Europe sorely lacks.

"Airbus passed Boeing in 2003 and looks to lead for the foreseeable future."

Airbus and Other European Companies Are Thriving Fair and Square

Floyd J. McKay

In the following viewpoint, Floyd J. McKay argues that Airbus's success can be attributed to a thriving and united Europe. While the United States is still concerned with building a bigger and better military, says McKay, the European Union (EU) is building a better standard of living for the citizens of its member states. McKay claims the Airbus is a symbol of this new sense of unity and progress. McKay is professor emeritus of journalism at Western Washington University.

As you read, consider the following questions:

1. What has changed about the status of European and American industries internationally, according to McKay?

2. According to the author, what is it about Airbus's origins that makes Americans scorn it?

3. What are Europeans building instead of armies, according to McKay?

The A380, the behemoth airliner rolled out recently by the Europeans, is not just about Boeing.

The Airbus Industries' mammoth jet is really all about Europe.

And Americans who have made fun of the "Old Europe"— [former U.S. secretary of defense] Donald Rumsfeld comes to mind—sooner or later must wake up and smell the fondue.

Increasingly, there is no "old Europe" or "new Europe." There is simply one Europe, and it is rapidly surpassing the United States in areas where we have long dominated.

Airplane manufacturing is just one of these areas; Airbus passed Boeing in 2003 and looks to lead for the foreseeable future.

As T.R. Reid points out in his excellent book, *The United States of Europe* (Penguin, 2004), a great deal of American business and industry is now owned by European firms, and the European Union is capable of checkmating American industries that formerly had been able to call the shots internationally.

It remains to be seen, of course, whether the A380 will dominate international travel as Boeing's aircraft have for many years. There is a "Spruce Goose" [overly large] look to the thing.

But Airbus Industries is a symbol of what is happening in Europe, with serious implications for American industry.

Airbus began as a government-financed effort to preserve Europe's airframe industry, with Britain, France and Germany cooperating in 1967 to form a counterweight to Boeing's domination of the field. It is now privately owned, and profitable.

Americans scorn this as "socialism," a term in bad odor in this country but widely accepted in Europe. We have our own

Boeing Has No Gripe Against Airbus

When the European upstart began to emerge as a serious competitor, Boeing executives complained loudly that Airbus was essentially an EU welfare project, kept alive by massive government loans and subsidies. This was true. A U.S. government study in 1990 showed that Airbus had received outright payments of about $13 billion from various European governments since its founding, and another $26 billion in loans. The Europeans could hardly deny that national governments and the EU itself had propped up Airbus in its early decades; indeed, Europe is proud of it. The pattern of governmental support for European firms competing in global markets is a hallmark of EU operations, one of the key strategies Brussels is using to further the industrial counterweight campaign. Even a national champion like Boeing could not keep up with a competitor that was skillfully riding the wave of European unification.

Even though its complaints were accurate, however, Boeing was hardly a sympathetic figure when it came to griping about government handouts. The U.S. champion has received billions of dollars of its own in research grants, tax breaks, and noncompetitive contracts from Washington. It has been a major beneficiary of the Buy American Act, a federal law that requires the world's largest government to buy all its aircraft from a domestic source—i.e., Boeing.

T.R. Reid, The United States of Europe: The New Superpower and the End of American Supremacy, *2004*.

forms of socialism, of course—no-bid contracts for Halliburton [a defense contractor investigated in a bribery scandal], tax giveaways and no-bid or rigged contracts for other defense contractors. We just don't call it socialism.

The combination of socialism and private enterprise is one of the tools Europe is using to compete with us, just as Japan has done with its close linkage of business and government.

Final assembly of the A380 was in Toulouse, France, following subcontracting in a dozen countries, a truly European effort. The idea that such a thing can occur on a continent that 60 years ago was a rubble heap of war and hatred is staggering.

America Focuses on War While the EU Is Raising the Standard of Living

What has happened in Europe is that an entire continent has turned its back on war and given up some of the trappings of nationalism in order to keep the peace. Americans simply don't understand the war-weariness of Europeans; the 20th century for Europe was one war after another, all fought on European soil.

This explains not only the commitment to working together but the general European reluctance to engage in American crusades, from Vietnam to Iraq. That front row of dignitaries unveiling the A380 was, with the notable exception of British Prime Minister Tony Blair, composed of adamant opponents of Bush administration foreign policy.

America has the military power to defeat any enemy, at least in the short term, but the cost of this militarism has been to divert billions of tax dollars into armaments, military personnel and defense contractors. This is the military-industrial complex that President Dwight Eisenhower warned of half a century ago.

Europe has basically turned its back on the military-industrial complex, thanks in no small part to our willingness (eagerness, even) to engage in wars to liberate and democratize on our terms. There is a European Union [EU] military force, and all EU nations maintain armed forces, but even to-gether they are dwarfed by our military might.

We are attempting to combat Islamic extremism with guns; EU nations are trying to accommodate their growing Muslim population and bring Turkey into the EU. Neither tactic is certain, but ours has been bloodier and costlier.

While we are building armies, Europe is building a standard of living that is in many ways superior to ours. Certainly, many Europeans have better health care, shorter work weeks, longer vacations and a stronger currency. The European press is free and vibrant, arts and culture flourish, and European cities attract rather than repel visitors.

The European debt to Americans is substantial—our entry into World War II saved democracy in Europe, and the Marshall Plan was critical to its rebuilding. Europeans have not forgotten these legacies, as witnessed most recently on 9/11 [September 11, 2001] when all of Europe grieved for America.

But Europe is not willing to be only a marketplace for American goods and an echo of American votes in the United Nations. The resolve of EU leaders to be a counterweight to American power is well illustrated with the unveiling of the A380.

Periodical Bibliography

The following articles have been selected to supplement the diverse views presented in this chapter.

Timothy Garton Ash   "The Great Powers of Europe, Redefined," *New York Times*, December 17, 2004.

Gerard Baker   "What America Can Do for Europe," *The Weekly Standard*, June 20, 2005.

Jose Manuel Barroso   "Hands Across the Ocean: EU—U.S. Summit," *International Herald Tribune*, April 27, 2007.

Tony Blair   "Europe Is Falling Behind," *Newsweek International*, November 28, 2005.

Andrea Broughton   "Enlargement Transforms EU Labour Market," *European Industrial Relations Review*, May 2004.

The Economist   "The Quest for Prosperity," March 17, 2007.

Michael Freedman   "Old World Opportunity," *Forbes*, July 25, 2005.

Peter Gumbel   "When Reform Doesn't Pay the Bills," *Time International*, October 23, 2006.

Floyd J. McKay   "EU Investments Lift the Scottish Highlands," *Seattle Times*, October 1, 2003.

Andrew Moravcsik   "The Golden Moment," *Newsweek International*, March 26, 2007.

Andreas Schleicher   "A Classless Act," *Newsweek International*, November 28, 2005.

Irwin M. Stelzer   "Of Morals and the Marketplace: How Protectionism—in All Its Many Forms—Affects the New Global Economy," *The Weekly Standard*, October 8, 2006.

Philip Terzian   "A Continent Made Up of Nations: In Europe, *e Pluribus Pluribus*," *The Weekly Standard*, June 20, 2005.

CHAPTER 4

What Should the EU Do About Its Diverse Nationalities and Languages?

Chapter Preface

One important change to take place in Europe due to the European Union (EU) has been greater movement of people. This is the goal of one arm of the pursuit of a single market: the freedom of access of people. While the current European Union struggles with developing a sense of a European identity and with the lack of a common language, these struggles may very well diminish in coming years as people become more mobile. Mobility may have the effect both of diminishing the importance of national identities and increasing the use of common languages.

Beginning in 1987, the ERASMUS program has provided millions of European students the chance to live and study in a foreign country, after completing one year of university study. The program encourages student and teacher mobility, and promotes transnational cooperation projects among universities across Europe. The potential countries of study, as of 2008, include all twenty-seven EU countries; the candidate countries of Switzerland and Turkey; and the three European Economic Area and European Free Trade Association (EEA-EFTA) countries of Iceland, Liechtenstein, and Norway.

The European Commission reports that students in the ERASMUS program increased their linguistic competence, with their ability to work in their second language increased "40% to 65% compared to those that did not participate in the ERASMUS mobility scheme." Additionally, a large number of students report that their time abroad allowed them "to start or improve their skills in a *third* or even a *fourth* foreign language." Additionally, many students end up living in the host country of study after their experience as a student. The ERASMUS program is creating a generation of young people who are multilingual and mobile.

The freedom of access of people throughout Europe created by the European Union allows for opportunities such as foreign study through the ERASMUS program. With people increasingly seeking study and employment outside of their own country, one can expect that the number of people speaking in a language other than their mother tongue and living in a country other than their own will only increase in the coming years. What this will do to Europeans' sense of the importance of their own nationality and native tongue remains to be seen.

In the following chapter, the authors debate the issue of diverse nationalities and languages, considering the compatibility of national identity and European identity, and considering the issue of a common language for Europeans.

"Open borders and changing demographics are slowly forging an identity that goes beyond a merely national one."

A European Identity Is Compatible with National Identity

Kyle James

In the following viewpoint, Kyle James argues that people across the European Union (EU), especially young people, are developing a European identity. Rather than replacing their national identities, James claims that the European identity exists alongside national identity in most cases. James believes the development of a stronger European identity will take time and will likely be based on values, rather than cultural characteristics. James is a journalist at Deutsche Welle, Germany's international broadcaster.

As you read, consider the following questions:

1. What percentage of European adults feel a solely national identity and what percentage feel some European identity, according to a recent survey by the European Union cited by the author?

2. What is the main historical reason that the author cites to support his view that it could take decades for a strong European identity to form?

3. What kinds of shared values does James suggest may help form a European identity in the future?

What binds Europeans together?

Europeans are both citizens of their own countries, and citizens of a European supranational union, the EU [European Union]. Which do they feel a real part of? Surveys show increasing numbers feel allegiance to both.

European lives can be so transnational, it's enough to make your head spin. But for many born in a member state of the EU, crossing borders for work, love or just for the adventure of it all is a simple, and very realizable fact of life.

National Identities Making Room for a European Identity

One might be born in Great Britain, but living in Brussels [Belgium] while working for a German company. Or a Swede might have moved to Edinburgh [Scotland] to go to university, started his career in Copenhagen [Denmark], then moved to Germany with his wife. As internal borders have become more porous for EU citizens, many are now comfortable living in countries other than those in which they were born.

Still, although he might often be seen eating *frites* at his favorite Brussels restaurant, the Briton might still feel very British and the Swede Swedish, although he himself gobbles down more *Currywurst* from Berlin street vendors than herring in Stockholm.

A "European" identity has not replaced national identities among EU citizens, although open borders and changing demographics are slowly forging an identity that goes beyond a merely national one.

"While the cultural formed identities are largely national ones, there is a European identity that is beginning to emerge" said Monika Mokre, deputy director of the Vienna-based Institute for European Integration Research.

Data Reflect Changing Attitudes

Data gathered by the European Union appear to confirm that. A 2004 survey by Eurobarometer found 42 percent of the population over the age of 18 said they felt themselves to be solely nationals of their own countries, while 58 percent indicated that they felt some European identification.

The same survey conducted in 1996 found that the numbers feeling at least some amount of "European-ness" along with their national identity were lower at each age group.

At one end of the scale in the 2004 survey was Luxembourg, where 17 percent of persons interviewed felt themselves to be solely European. At the other end was newer member Hungary, where almost two-thirds (64 percent) of those asked said they felt only Hungarian. Germany fell somewhere in the middle.

Age also plays a role. The older the respondents, the more they consider themselves as only citizens of their own countries. The younger the person, the more likely they are to see themselves now or in the near future as citizens of their own country and, at the same time, European citizens.

"Young people tend to look beyond their own borders more than older people do," said Mokre. "This has partly to do with better communication methods, such as the internet"

Developing a European Identity Will Take Time

Forging an EU identity has been a slow process, and experts say it could be decades before the strong European identity becomes anchored in large swaths of the populace.

There are historical reasons for that, according to Markus Hadler, an associate professor of sociology at the University of

Decline in National Identity Is a Positive Sign of Globalism

Among Europeans and people of other regions around the world, national pride is declining with each successive generation. America is the exception. A whopping 98 percent of American youth report being proud of their nationality, compared with only 58 percent of British youth and 65 percent of German youth. Most Americans see these numbers as a positive sign of the vitality of the republic. Many Europeans wonder if America is lost in the past. In a globalizing era where allegiance to country is becoming less important in defining individual and collective identity, the fact that Americans remain so passionately committed to the conventional nation-state political model puts us squarely on the side of traditional geopolitics, but hardly of a new global consciousness.

Jeremy Rifkin,
The European Dream, *2004.*

Graz in Austria. For many centuries in Europe, the nation state was the main reference point. The EU's founding was a move made by politicians to guarantee peace and promote economic development in a Europe that had been torn apart by war. It was not a grass-roots effort, nor a particularly exciting or dramatic one.

"Europe lacks a founding myth, like other countries," he said. "Everybody knows about the Boston Tea Party, but there's nothing similar in Europe. Tea parties in Brussels are very different."

But in much political science literature identity with a political system is regarded as necessary for its long-term stability and legitimacy. The identification leads the citizen to act as a community member and reflects an emotional attachment to the system.

That identification is important, experts say, since it acts as a stepping stone in the ongoing integration process and could help "uphold" the process in times of crisis.

"If we want a democratic EU, identity is important" said Mokre. "It's necessary that citizens in the end stand together with this new kind of governing form."

Attitudes and Values Will Create This Identity

Identity can be a fuzzy thing, however, and although more EU citizens are feeling somewhat "European" these days, it is not all together clear just exactly what it is they are feeling. Cultural differences in Europe are so pronounced that it is unlikely a Portuguese farmer just outside Porto is going to think he has much in common with the Polish plumber near the border to Belarus.

But an EU identity is based [upon] and will likely further develop along a broad range of political and social attitudes and values that are separate from those cultural characteristics by which people define themselves, according to several experts.

Those values could be a strong belief in democracy and human rights, a certain amount of social fairness, the separation of church and state, and a fairly widespread view on the role of government, according to Katinka Barysch of the Center for European Reform.

"For example, a kind of social system you have in the United States where millions of people are without health insurance would be unacceptable to most Europeans," she said.

Some feared that the debacle with the EU Constitution, which France and the Netherlands rejected in referenda, and the enlargement of the bloc from 15 to 25 states in 2004 and then to 27 states in 2007, would set back the formation of a common identity. Many of the newer member countries have very different cultural and political backgrounds than older states and the constitution rejection appeared to some to put the entire EU project in question.

"At least in these cases, there was a real debate going on about Europe," said Mokre. "Having a European identity doesn't mean you have to think everything about the EU is just fantastic."

*"National identity is one of the most te-
nacious of human feelings."*

There Is No European
Identity, Only
National Identity

Daniel Hannan

*In the following viewpoint, Daniel Hannan argues that there is
no European identity because the European Union (EU) lacks a
history that creates identity. Furthermore, Hannan claims it is
this lack of identity, and associated lack of patriotism, which has
created so many problems for the EU. Hannan argues that none
of the current strategies being pursued by the EU can artificially
create this identity that the EU needs to succeed. Hannan is a
conservative member of parliament for South East England.*

As you read, consider the following questions:

1. What does identity have to do with willingness to accept
   the euro, according to the author?

2. What specific problem in the European Union does
   Hannan argue is the result of a lack of Euro-patriotism?

Daniel Hannan, "No Anthem Will Make Us Love Europe," *Daily Telegraph*, May 19,
2002. www.telegraph.co.uk. Reproduced by permission.

3. What point about the European Union does Hannan
want to make by discussing the failure of the USSR
(Union of Soviet Socialist Republics) to create a Soviet
identity?

Do you get a lump in your throat when you hear the words
of [Friedrich von] Schiller's Ode to Joy [the European
Union (EU) anthem]? Do you grow misty-eyed at the mention of our great European heroes, [the EU founders] Robert
Schuman, Alcide de Gasperi and Jean Monnet? Do you blink
back the tears when you see the blue and gold Stars [of the
EU flag] being waved at the Ryder Cup [golf tournament between U.S. and EU players]?

I thought not. And that, according to [EU commissioner
for external relations] Chris Patten, is the trouble. "A healthy
European democracy will develop only when people begin to
feel an emotional attachment to their European identity," says
Our Man in Brussels in the current issue of *The Spectator*.

There Is No European Identity

One sees his point. The reason that we feel closer to our nations than to the EU is not simply that the EU often does
things badly; it is also because the nations are able to draw on
a deep well of sentiment: of poetry and literature, of national
heroes, of history. The EU offers us the trappings of statehood—flag, passport, anthem—with no underlying sense of
common identity.

The timing of the Commissioner's comments is interesting. [British prime minister] Tony Blair has made it clear that
he wants a referendum on the euro [the EU's common monetary unit] next year [in 2003]. He has also made clear how
he intends to fight it. He will present the question, as he did
to [journalist] Jeremy Paxman on Wednesday [May 14, 2002],
as a wholly economic one, and make a great song and dance
out of pretending to have met the Treasury's five tests.

Mr Patten implicitly disagrees. For him, the matter has as much to do with heart as with head. In this, he is reflecting the prevailing view in Brussels [Belgium, headquarters of the EU's executive branch], which has always held the euro to be a political goal, for which the EU should be prepared to pay an economic price. He is no doubt aware that the countries where the new currency has been most enthusiastically embraced—Belgium, Italy, Luxembourg—are also those whose people are readiest to identify themselves as "Europeans".

Lack of European Identity Has Caused Problems

I see Mr Patten in Brussels from time to time, mooching around disconsolately. He seems somehow greyer and paunchier than when he arrived, and the bags under his eyes have spread. Not long ago, it was reported that he was "counting the hours" until the end of his term. I put it down to disillusionment. To a man like Mr Patten, a principled and idealistic European, the reality of the Brussels system must be hard to bear. Instead of finding himself among pioneers, working to transcend war and bring a new political order to the continent, he has found himself among some of the most stubborn and self-serving officials in Europe. Even his thoroughly uncontentious plans to make the EU's overseas aid programme less corrupt ran up against vested interests in the bureaucracy. We sceptics are not really surprised when the EU makes a mess of things. We may kick up a fuss about the expenses regime, or about the billions of unspent euros in the budget, or about fraud. But, inside, we are enjoying the warm glow that comes from having our prejudices confirmed.

For Mr Patten, the failings of the Brussels system are far more painful. He is desperate to make it work, and believes that this could be achieved by generating a sense of civic loyalty. As long as no one feels any Euro-patriotism, people will treat the EU largely as an opportunity to get their hands on public money.

The trouble is that nationhood cannot be created overnight by bureaucratic fiat. Nations evolve because their citizens feel enough in common one with another to accept government from each other's hands. This identity may be shaped by many things: language, culture, history, or geography. But it cannot simply be synthesized.

The EU's Attempts to Forge an Identity Are Futile

The EU's attempts to "strengthen the sense of European citizenship" range from the irritating to the hilarious. As well as the passport and the driving licence, there are proposals for a single EU international [dialing] code, and for a common internet address: dot eu. There is also an EU public holiday, Europe day, which fell, as you were doubtless aware, . . . [on May 9, 2002].

And then there is Ode to Joy to which, at least in Brussels, we are now expected to stand to attention (I find that it has the same effect on me as on Alex in *A Clockwork Orange* [for violent and ecstatic release], and for the same reason: bad connotations). The idea that these and similar gestures will make us feel European, in the same way that someone feels American or Norwegian, is preposterous.

National identity is one of the most tenacious of human feelings. The USSR tried for 70 years to give its people a sense of Soviet nationality. Yet, as soon as they were free to vote, they reverted to their traditional linguistic units. I can already hear the Europhiles spluttering into their sancerre. There is nothing that annoys them more than mention of the European and Soviet Unions in the same context. But I am not trying to argue that the EU is a totalitarian system. On the contrary, my point is that not even the Soviet Union, with all the resources of a police state at its disposal, was able to extirpate the older patriotisms of its peoples. How, then, can the EU, made up of 15 liberal democracies, hope to succeed with nothing more powerful in its arsenal than a common passport?

Mr Patten thinks he has the answer. "You can already feel the stirrings [of pro-European patriotism], perhaps, in the shared indignation at US steel protection," he writes. "You can feel it at the Ryder Cup, too." It is significant that the only two examples he can come up with are based on anti-Americanism. From his point of view, this may make tactical sense. Nations do indeed cohere when they perceive an external enemy. And there is a certain market for anti-Americanism even in this country. But I wonder whether long exile is beginning to distort Mr Patten's view of the British.

When truly important matters are at stake, we tend to sympathise most with the community of free English-speaking nations, the countries which have stuck by us in most conflicts from the First World War onwards.

No number of Ryder Cups can compete with the reality of cultural affinity, based on common legal and political traditions and, above all, on a shared language. Mr Patten shrewdly understands that a common EU identity will be facilitated by a sense of "them" and "us". But I suspect he will be disappointed by how the British define "us".

"With further countries soon to join the EU, some analysts fear the effectiveness of its institutions could be getting lost in translation."

The European Union's Many Official Languages Create Challenges

James Owen

In the following viewpoint, James Owen claims that the number of official languages of the European Union (EU) is creating problems. Owen argues that the accuracy of translation from one language to another is a primary concern. In addition, the author notes that finding translators to perform the translations is not always possible. Despite the official stance of the European Union of accommodating many languages, Owen argues that, in practice, people are moving more toward using a dominant language. Owen writes for National Geographic News.

As you read, consider the following questions:

1. According to the author, what sorts of practical needs do the language requirements of the European Union entail, in terms of translators, interpreters, and costs?

James Owen, "With 20 Official Languages, Is EU Lost in Translation?" *National Geographic News*, February 22, 2005. http://news.nationalgeographic.com. Reproduced by permission.

2. What official EU language went without a translator recently due to an inability to fill the position, according to Owen?

3. What language does the author claim is becoming the unofficial dominant language of the European Union?

The European Union [EU] has been operating in 20 official languages since ten new member states joined the legislative body last year [2004]. With annual translation costs set to rise to 1.3 billion dollars (U.S.), some people question whether EU institutions are becoming overburdened by multilingualism.

The Demands of So Many Languages

Brussels, Belgium, the European Union's headquarters city, is fast getting a reputation as the new Babel [the tower in the Bible's book of Genesis whose production was halted due to a confusion of languages]. Parliamentary sessions are conducted [in] 20 languages simultaneously. With further countries soon to join the EU, some analysts fear the effectiveness of its institutions could be getting lost in translation.

Czech, Estonian, Hungarian, Latvian, Lithuanian, Maltese, Polish, Slovak, and Slovene are the most recent tongues to become official EU languages. With the countries of Bulgaria, Croatia, and Romania also on the EU membership waiting list, the body is due to accommodate several more languages by 2010.

Even before expansion in 2004, the EU ran the world's largest translation operation—twice as big as that of the United Nations, which has six official languages.

EU institutions currently require around 2,000 written-text translators. They also need 80 interpreters per language per day, half of which operate at the European Parliament. The total annual cost of EU multilingualism will soon rise from 875 million dollars U.S. (670 million euros) to 1.3 billion dollars U.S. (1 billion euros), according to the European Commission, the union's executive body.

The European Parliament requires some 60 interpreters to help elected politicians from the 25 member states understand each other. These interpreters work in soundproofed booths, translating the words of European members of Parliament (MEPs). Even so, unfamiliar words or phrases can leave interpreters lost for words, says Struan Stevenson, a British MEP.

Lost in Translation

Referring to a debate last month [January 2005], Stevenson said, "The system ground to a sudden halt when a British MEP described the EU Constitution as 'gobbledygook.' Apparently there is no such word in Polish and some of the other East European languages. The interpreters were flummoxed—and that's another word they'd find hard to tackle."

Comic misunderstandings can arise that become part of Brussels lore. For instance, during an agricultural working group session, "frozen semen" was translated into French as "frozen seamen."

Another MEP recalls how the expression "out of sight, out of mind" became "invisible lunatic" after a computer-aided translation.

On a more serious note, Stevenson said, "Because it is deemed a fundamental right to be able to communicate with your electors in [your] own tongue, the parliament now has to work in 20 different languages. This exercise currently consumes tens of thousands of tons of paper a year, as every word spoken has to be typed up and filed in mountainous archives."

The European Commission (EC), the legislative body of the European Union, says it's essential that legislation is published in the official languages of all member states, because EU citizens can't be expected to comply with laws they don't understand.

Translation Should Be Limited

There are three fields in which all the languages should be given equal value:

• Functioning of the European parliament, as . . . the right of election should not be restricted to those who speak some languages.

• Information to the citizens [including] the programs and the legislation directed to the citizens. . . .

• All the citizens should have the right to address in their own language any of the EU institutions or offices, and to get the answer in their language. But these three points do no include all the documents the EU produces.

Bojan Brezigar, AMARAUNA World Languages Network,
December 2003.

However, the resulting translation workload has meant problems for both the EC and individual member states. For instance, Estonia's government this month reported major difficulties in ratifying some European legislation because of poor translation of EU laws.

Finding Translators

The EC also admits to difficulties in finding sufficient numbers of qualified translators in languages such as Maltese, which is spoken by only about 370,000 people.

Richard Rowe, spokesperson for the EC's Directorate-General for Translation, says the legal requirement that all EU legislation is simultaneously published in all official languages has been suspended until enough Maltese-speaking translators can be trained.

"Apart from the problem of the lack of qualified candidates for some languages, we are under budgetary constraints, which means we cannot recruit all the translators we need in an ideal world until 2006," Rowe added.

Yet the spokesman said the EC is taking measures to speed up and simplify its written translation work, which last year amounted to more than 1.5 million pages.

"One simplification measure the commission has already adopted is to impose a reduction in the length of texts sent to us for translation," he noted. Now these texts should not exceed 15 pages in length.

Most EC translators also have access to a powerful computer application called Translator's Workbench, which stores all previous work.

"The translator faced with a new assignment feeds it into the system and gets back a text in which the memory suggests translations of phrases, sentences, or even whole paragraphs [that] have been translated in the past," Rowe said. "We always recycle previous work wherever possible."

Moving Toward a Dominant Language

He adds that internal EC work is conducted largely in just three languages—English, French, and German—for reasons of efficiency and economy. In the longer term, such an approach may be the way forward throughout the EU, according to Giles Chichester, a British MEP.

"In practice, the institutions are trying to move towards one dominant language, with one or two other working languages," he said. "Let nature take its course."

Unofficially English is the language of choice within the EU. It is now used for drafting around 60 percent of all paperwork. English is also widely spoken as a second language in Europe, especially in Scandinavian and Eastern European countries. In Malta, the vast majority of residents understand English.

Officially, however, an EU dominated by English would be unacceptable politically. The French are particularly sensitive to its increased use, while multilingualism is considered a vital cornerstone of the European Parliament.

"Members are elected and represent the public because of their political stances, not their language skills," said Rowe, the EC translation-services spokesman. "So in the interests of democracy and transparency, the service provided to them has to be much more multilingual."

In fact, the amount of translation and interpretation work could multiply further if various political groups get their way. Catalan is spoken by some seven million Europeans, mostly in Spain. Yet it doesn't have official status within the EU. Similarly, the Irish and Welsh are lobbying for official recognition of their native Celtic tongues. [The Irish language was officially recognized as of June 2005.]

For the European Union to work as one, "Eurobabble" may be the price it has to pay.

"No other body at regional or global level uses as many official languages as the European Union."

The European Union's Many Official Languages Are Necessary

European Commission

In the following viewpoint, the European Commission gives its justification for why there must be so many official languages within the European Union (EU). Citing facts about the diverse languages of its members, the commission argues that the principles of democracy require that its members be able to participate in their own language. The European Commission is the executive branch of the European Union.

As you read, consider the following questions:

1. According to the European Commission, what is the minimum number of national languages guaranteed to each member country of the European Union?

European Commission, "Many Tongues, One Family: Languages in the European Union," July 2004. http://ec.europa.eu/publications/booklets/move/45/index_en.htm. Excerpts reproduced with kind permission of the European Commission from the original language edition published by the Office for Official Publications of the European Communities. Copyright © 2004 European Communities. Responsibility for the reproduction lies entirely with Cengage Learning.

2. Why are there fewer official languages than there are countries in the EU?

3. In what way does having so many official languages contribute to the democracy of the European Union, according to the European Commission?

The language we speak helps define who we are. The European Union [EU] respects this right to identity of its 450 million citizens. While committed to integration between its member states, the EU also actively promotes the freedom of its peoples to speak and write their own language. The two aims are complementary, embodying the EU's motto of *United in diversity*.

In addition, the Union actively encourages its citizens to learn other European languages, both for reasons of professional and personal mobility within its single market, and as a force for cross-cultural contacts and mutual understanding. In an ever-growing and more diverse EU, it is important that its citizens can communicate with each other. The Union also promotes the use of regional or minority languages which are not official EU languages, but which are spoken by up to 50 million people in the member countries, and as such form part of our cultural heritage.

Meeting Language Needs

The EU as an organisation operates in 20 official languages [as of July 2004]. Each country decides, when joining the European Union, which of its national languages it wishes to be used as an official EU language or languages. The complete list of the European Union's official languages is then agreed by all the EU governments. It thus includes at least one of the national languages of each country.

This means EU citizens can use their national language when dealing with the EU institutions, just as they can when dealing with their national authorities at home. Similarly, all legislation adopted by the EU is directly accessible to each citizen in his or her national language.

No other body at regional or global level uses as many official languages as the European Union. No other body spends so much on translation and interpretation, although the cost remains surprisingly modest. But then, no other body or grouping adopts legislation which applies directly to citizens in all its member states the way the EU does.

The 2004 enlargement of the EU, which nearly doubled the number of official languages from 11 to 20, focused attention on the role of languages in the EU as never before. . . .

The care the EU takes to sustain its linguistic diversity provides an eloquent response to those critics who allege that the Union is bent on erasing national or regional characteristics and imposing a 'European' uniformity.

Languages of the European Union

The languages of the EU come from a wide variety of roots. Most are members of the vast Indo-European group, whose main branches are Germanic, Romance, Slav and Celtic. Greek and the Baltic languages, Lithuanian and Latvian, are also Indo-European, although not part of any of the principal branches. Hungarian, Finnish and Estonian come from the Finno-Ugrian group of languages. Maltese is close to Arabic with Italian influences.

Most of the 'regional' and 'minority' languages in the EU also belong to one or another of the above groups. A principal exception is Basque, spoken on both sides of the Franco-Spanish border, whose roots are still being researched. The notion of 'minority' language covers not only lesser-used languages like the Sami language of Lapland or Breton in France, but also the use of official EU languages when spoken by a minority in another member country.

The 20 official EU languages are Czech, Danish, Dutch, English, Estonian, Finnish, French, German, Greek, Hungar-

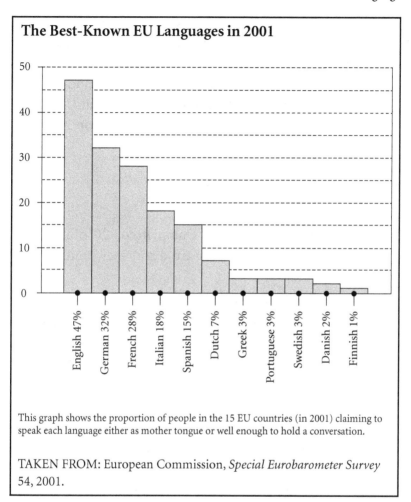

The Best-Known EU Languages in 2001

This graph shows the proportion of people in the 15 EU countries (in 2001) claiming to speak each language either as mother tongue or well enough to hold a conversation.

TAKEN FROM: European Commission, *Special Eurobarometer Survey* 54, 2001.

ian, Italian, Latvian, Lithuanian, Maltese, Polish, Portuguese, Slovak, Slovenian, Spanish and Swedish.

Celtic languages are spoken in the western confines of Europe—Ireland, Brittany in France and western parts of the United Kingdom. None is an official language of the European Union. However, Irish Gaelic has a special status: the EU treaties and some key texts have been translated into this language, which can also be used by Irish citizens for certain contacts with the EU institutions.

The EU has fewer official languages than member countries. This is because Germany and Austria share German, the United Kingdom and Ireland use the same language. Greece and Cyprus share Greek, and Belgium and Luxembourg have common languages with their French, Dutch and German neighbours. The result is 20 official languages for 25 countries. . . .

Democracy in the EU Requires Many Languages

The reasons why the European Union needs 20 official languages are not hard to find: they are democracy, transparency and the right to know.

EU legislation applies throughout the EU, and therefore to all its citizens. New legislation must be published and made available to them in their own language. As in any democracy, each citizen has a fundamental right to know why a particular item of legislation is being adopted and what it requires him or her to do.

It is also a basic tenet of the European Union that all its citizens and their elected representatives must have the same right of access to the EU and be able to communicate with its institutions and authorities in their national language. There cannot be double standards, say, between big and small countries or between those with well-known and lesser-known languages.

Latvian or Greek members of the European Parliament must be able to speak on behalf of their voters in their own language in the same way as a member from Germany, Britain or France. The same holds good for a government minister at an official EU meeting or a citizen who takes a grievance to the European Ombudsman. The 14% of Irish citizens who consider Irish Gaelic as their mother tongue can use it to complain to the Ombudsman if they so wish.

Its law-making function and the direct involvement of its citizens explain why the EU uses more languages than multinational bodies like the United Nations or NATO [North Atlantic Treaty Organization], which operate only at the intergovernmental level. Although it has more than 190 members, the UN [United Nations] uses only six languages. The Council of Europe and NATO, each with more members than the EU, publish official documents only in English and French.

The EU institutions have therefore honed procedures over the years for operating in a rising number of official languages without creating a veritable Tower of Babel [the structure featured in the Bible's book of Genesis whose creation was halted due to a confusion of languages]. They have also striven to give citizens and governments quality translation and interpretation efficiently and cheaply.

▌ *"French is best for precision."*

French Should Be the Official Language of the European Union

Dan Bilefsky

In the following viewpoint, Dan Bilefsky reports on a proposal by Maurice Druon, who argues that the European Union (EU) should have one dominant language and that this language ought to be French. Druon claims that the French language is uniquely suited to the purpose of being the official language of legal documents. Druon is a French novelist and member of the French Academy, the institution for issues pertaining to the French language. Bilefsky writes for the New York Times *and the* International Herald Tribune.

As you read, consider the following questions:

1. According to the author, what key figures have joined Maurice Druon's campaign to make French the supreme language of the European Union?

2. According to Bilefsky, what three languages are used for the first drafts of EU documents?

Dan Bilefsky, "Linguistic Don Quixote Comes to Brussels," *International Herald Tribune*, March 1, 2007. www.iht.com. Reprinted with permission.

3. According to the author, why does Druon believe French is superior to English for use in the legal documents of the European Union?

A n elder statesman of French literature who fought for the Resistance in World War II is gearing up to do battle again, in Brussels [Belgium, headquarters of the European Union (EU)]: Maurice Druon, 89, is campaigning to make French the supreme language of legal documents in the European Union.

Droun's Proposal

A member of the Académie Française and the author of 60 books, Druon has been joined in this initiative by an unlikely assortment of Francophiles, politicians and aristocrats— among them Nicole Fontaine, a former president of the European Parliament; Otto von Habsburg, a descendant of the German royal house; Antoinette Spaak, daughter of Paul-Henri Spaak, a founding father of the EU and once a Belgian foreign minister; and Bronislaw Geremek, a Polish historian.

They support his proposal that French should become the deciding language when there are differences over what a legal document actually means—all the more so in an expanded EU of 27 countries, where French is struggling to retain its historic primacy alongside the EU's 22 other official languages, including Maltese and Gaelic.

"Italian is the language of song, German is the language of philosophy and English is good for poetry, but French is best for precision," Druon said of his quest. "French should be the authoritative language for law because it is related to Latin—in which Roman law was written—and it was also the language of the Napoleonic Code."

Druon's battle is open-ended—there is no deadline or crucial vote looming—but he wants resolution before the EU gets bigger and even more linguistically cumbersome.

The Official EU Languages

The 23 official languages of the EU are Bulgarian, Czech, Danish, German, Estonian, Greek, English, Spanish, French, Irish, Italian, Latvian, Lithuanian, Hungarian, Maltese, Dutch, Polish, Portuguese, Romanian, Slovak, Slovene, Finnish, and Swedish.

The EU comprises 489 million people, who are trying to speak with one voice while maintaining a Babel of languages and cultural identities. In order not to offend any one country, the EU uses each of the 22 languages spoken in member states, at a cost each year of as much as €1.2 billion, or $1.6 billion, in translation and interpretation expenses.

Why French Is a Better Choice than English

Every country is entitled to have EU documents translated into its native language, although to save time the first draft of documents, including legal material, is often available only in one of the Union's unofficial working languages: English, French and German.

Druon, who recently came to Brussels to lobby EU officials, insisted that he was no cultural nationalist and recalled, in broken but colorful English, that he learned to love the queen's language as a soldier in wartime London.

"I love English," he said, "though I now call it 'Anglo-American' because we no longer speak British English due to globalization and America's economic power." But Anglophilia aside, Druon remains steadfast that the language of [French political philosopher] Montesquieu is the superior language for legal discourse. He notes that it is no coincidence that the EU's highest court, the European Court of Justice in Luxembourg, uses French, not English, as its working language: French has fewer syntactical ambiguities, he said.

Critics say that the offensive of the Druon committee—officially the Committee for the Language of European Law—smacks of desperation and reflects an effort by France to reassert itself amid signs that its influence in the European Union is waning.

"It sounds nice to French ears, but let's get real—we are living in the 21st century and English is the language that everyone understands," huffed an EU official, who nevertheless declined to use his last name for fear of offending Gallic sensitivities and Druon in particular, whom he called "a French monument."

An EU official from France added that the initiative was strictly that of a private individual and did not reflect his government's policy—although Druon said that he had discussed the idea with President Jacques Chirac and other top officials and that they had offered encouragement.

To buttress French in relation to other languages, and English in particular, France offered the EU's newest commissioners from the east a free crash course in the language at a chateau near Avignon after the EU's expansion in May 2004. But a survey of officials from the new member states found that 69 percent used English as their second language, followed by German, then French.

Paul-Marie Couteaux, a French member of the European Parliament for the Mouvement Pour la France, which defends French rights, said that the dominance of English in the EU meant that non-English-speaking members of Parliament often had no understanding of the documents they were reading or voting on. Moreover, he argued, something gets lost in translation when the EU attempts simultaneous interpretation among all of its recognized languages—for example, from Maltese to English to French.

"We French don't often speak English and often don't understand it, so this creates confusion," said Couteaux, who was a speechwriter at the United Nations and speaks impeccable English. "We French were not elected because of our ability to speak English."

Pietro Petrucci, the EU spokesman for multilingualism—a new post created to help the bloc grapple with its growing cacophony of languages—emphasized that no legislation could become law until it had been translated into all EU languages, although he acknowledged that translation backlogs sometimes created delays.

He also noted that in many ways Druon's aim had been achieved: If there are differences of legal interpretation in the EU, disputes are resolved at the European Court of Justice, whose working language is French. "The rule that EU laws must be available in all of the community's languages, and that all languages are equal, has been the rule of the club for half a century," he said. "Any efforts to resist this will face difficulties."

Periodical Bibliography

The following articles have been selected to supplement the diverse views presented in this chapter.

The Economist	"After Babel, a New Common Tongue," August 7, 2004.
European Report	"EU Languages: After Gaelic, What Next?" July 28, 2006.
Jon Henley	"A Very French Row," *World Press Review,* May 2004.
Brian Hindo	"What's 'Trade Union' in Catalan?" *Business Week,* January 10, 2005.
Irish Times	"Equality Is Central to Social Cohesion, the Economy and Greater Democracy," June 7, 2004.
Stryker McGuire	"Britain's Big Tent: The Real 'New Europe' Is an Arc of Countries that Share a Very English Approach to the Region," *Newsweek International,* September 27, 2004.
Owen Matthews	"Sliding Backward: An Ugly Nationalist Mood Is Brewing in Ankara, Stalling Once Hailed Reforms," *Newsweek International,* April 24, 2006.
Brandon Mitchener	"Silence, Please: It's Time to Sing the EU Anthem," *The Wall Street Journal,* May 7, 2003.
John O'Sullivan	"In Defense of Nationalism," *The National Interest,* Winter 2004.
John Tagliabue	"Soon, Europe Will Speak in 23 Tongues," *New York Times,* December 6, 2006.
William Underhill	"EU: Parlez-vous Maltese?" *Newsweek,* March 22, 2004.
Jonathan Yim	"Feasability of the Language Policy of the European Union," *International Lawyer,* Spring 2007.

For Further Discussion

Chapter 1

1. Jeffrey Kopstein identifies three challenges the European Union (EU) currently faces. Timothy Garton Ash proposes six shared goals that he believes should define Europe in the future. How do you think the pursuit of these six goals would either help or make worse the challenges identified by Kopstein? Explain your answer.

2. Gary Younge believes that the failure of the proposed constitution was, in part, a response to a lack of democracy in the EU institutions. In what way or ways do you think the European Union is democratic? In what way or ways do you think it is undemocratic?

3. Both Patrick Buchanan and Charles Kupchan raise concerns about how nationalism in EU member states is a challenge for the development of a European Union identity. Within the United States, people appear to be able to have an identity as a member of a particular state (e.g., California) while also having a national identity, without conflict. In what ways are the United States and the European Union similar and different, and how do you think this affects the ability of their respective citizens to have identities that involve both that of a local state member and member of a larger union?

Chapter 2

1. The viewpoints of both Hans-Juergen Zahorka and *The Economist* point to the ambiguity of using the criterion of being "European" as necessary for entry into the European Union, since the term may refer to geography or values.

For each of the two understandings of "European," identify the countries that you believe could be a part of the European Union under that definition.

2. Tom Spencer argues that if Turkey is allowed to join the European Union, then there would be no good reason for denying entrance to Morocco, Armenia, Algeria, and so on. Is this a good argument for keeping out Turkey or is it a slippery-slope fallacy? Explain your answer.

3. Vernon Coleman expresses his view that the United Kingdom of Great Britain (England, Scotland, and Wales) and Northern Ireland should leave the European Union. Focusing on the specific reasons he gives for his view, provide responses to his concerns from the viewpoint of Richard Laming. What do you think Coleman would say about Laming's responses?

Chapter 3

1. Robert Kagan argues that although it would be beneficial for the United States to "pay its respects to multilateralism" by involving the European Union in its global security strategy, Kagan concludes that the United States does not actually need the European Union in order to maintain global security. Ronald D. Asmus and Kenneth M. Pollack disagree, claiming that the United States needs to develop a joint strategy with the European Union in order to be successful in key places like the Middle East. After reading both viewpoints, with what position do you agree? Use textual support to back up your answer.

2. Both Richard W. Rahn and Olivier J. Blanchard cite the fact that the average European Union citizen has about two-thirds the income, gross domestic product (GDP), or purchasing power parity (PPP) of the average U.S. citizen. How does each author apply this fact to reach divergent conclusions about how well the economy of the European Union is doing?

3. Bruce Bartlett concludes that Europeans do not work as much as Americans because of the high taxes they pay. What alternate explanation might Olivier J. Blanchard and Thomas Geoghegan give for why Europeans work less than Americans?

4. The view of the *Investor's Business Daily* is that Airbus has received government subsidies, precluding fair competition with Boeing. What sort of similarly socialist practices in the United States does Floyd J. McKay cite in objection to this kind of criticism of Europe's business practices? How do you think the *Investor's Business Daily* would respond to McKay?

Chapter 4

1. Kyle James believes Europeans are developing a European identity alongside their particular national identities, whereas Daniel Hannan does not believe a rich European identity is possible without a more substantial shared history. What do you think would hasten the development of a European identity?

2. James Owen argues that the practice of allowing many official languages of the European Union creates problems, whereas the European Commission argues that it is necessary to have all the languages. Some, like Dan Bilefsky, believe there should be only one official language of the European Union. Given the vast number of languages spoken in Europe, with no one language being spoken by all, what policy should the European Union adopt to balance fairness and efficacy? Justify your answer.

Organizations to Contact

The editors have compiled the following list of organizations concerned with the issues debated in this book. The descriptions are derived from materials provided by the organizations. All have publications or information available for interested readers. The list was compiled on the date of publication of the present volume; the information provided here may change. Readers need to remember that many organizations take several weeks or longer to respond to inquiries.

Centre for European Reform (CER)
14 Great College St., Westminster, London   SW1P 3RX
United Kingdom
44-2072331199 • fax: 44-2072331117
e-mail: info@cer.org.uk
Web site: www.cer.org.uk

The CER regards integration as beneficial, but aims to promote new ideas for reforming the European Union. The CER organizes seminars, conferences, and meetings, bringing together leaders in politics and business. A result of their research and seminars are multiple publications, including *The U.S. Elections and Europe: The Coming Crisis of High Expectations.*

EurActiv
International Press Centre, 1 Bd. Charlemagne, boîte 1
Brussels   B-1041
Belgium
32-22265810 • fax: 32-22265820
Web site: www.euractiv.com

EurActiv brings together the skills of professionals with experience in European Union (EU) affairs, journalism, information, and communication to provide an independent media portal dedicated to opening debate about EU policies.

EurActiv's coverage of EU affairs concentrates on policy positions by EU actors trying to influence policies in the prelegislative phase. The Web site includes news and information about a variety of EU topics, including enlargement, climate change, public affairs, trade, and transport.

EUROPA—Gateway to the European Union
European Commission, Brussels   B-1049
   Belgium
32-22999696
Web site: www.europa.eu

EUROPA is the European Union's portal Web site, administered by the European Commission. EUROPA provides a vast array of information on European integration, particularly concerning the European Union's objectives, policies, and institutional setup. Numerous publications are available at the site including the *Official Journal*, published daily, and the text of numerous official documents, including the full texts of the European Treaties.

European Centre for Public Affairs (ECPA)
Brunel University Business School, Uxbridge
Middlesex   UB8 3PH
   United Kingdom
44-8704442760 • fax: 44-8704442770
e-mail: ecpa@publicaffairs.ac
Web site: www.publicaffairs.ac

The ECPA is a nonprofit organization that works closely with the European Commission, the European Parliament, and the Presidency of the European Union to develop understanding of the evolving process of governing Europe. The ECPA develops customized programs on a wide range of public affairs issues for companies and organizations. Among the publications available at their Web site is *Europe Needs an FBI.*

European Policy Centre (EPC)
Residence Palace, 155 rue de la Loi, Brussels   B-1040
   Belgium
32-22310340 • fax: 32-22310704
e-mail: info@epc.eu
Web site: www.epc.eu

The EPC is an independent, not-for-profit think tank, committed to making European integration work. The EPC makes policy recommendations resulting from debates on the issues of EU integration and citizenship, Europe's political economy, and Europe in the world. The EPC publishes policy briefs and issue papers, including *EU-Turkey Relations 43 Years On: Train Crash or Temporary Derailment?*, available at their Web site.

Global Policy Forum Europe (GPF Europe)
Bertha-von-Suttner-Platz 13, Bonn   D-52111
   Germany
49-2289650510 • fax: 49-2289638206
e-mail: europe@globalpolicy.org
Web site: www.globalpolicy.org/eu

GPF Europe is a nonprofit organization in Germany that monitors and analyzes European policy making relating to and within the United Nations (UN). GPF Europe initiatives involve developmental politics, UN reform, and corporate accountability. Among its publications is the yearly *Social Watch Report*, available at their Web site.

Open Europe
7 Tufton St., London   SW1P 3QN
   United Kingdom
44-2071972333 • fax: 44-2071972307
e-mail: info@openeurope.org.uk
Web site: www.openeurope.org.uk

Open Europe is an independent think tank set up by some of the United Kingdom's leading businesspeople to contribute new thinking to the debate about the direction of the EU. Open Europe seeks to disseminate ideas about the European

Union that embrace radical reform based on economic liberalization, a looser and more flexible structure, and greater transparency and accountability. Among its publications available at its Web site is *A Guide to the Constitutional Treaty.*

The Robert Schuman Foundation
29, bd Raspail, Paris   F-75007
   France
33-153638300
e-mail: info@robert-schuman.eu
Web site: www.robert-schuman.eu

The Robert Schuman Foundation was founded in 1991 and works to promote the construction of Europe both with regard to its ideas and in the field alongside the citizens themselves. The foundation performs research to provide European decision makers with information and helps new member states with integration. Among its many publications are *Nationalism and Religion in the Western Balkans—The March of the Western Balkans towards the European Union* and *Europe—United States: Common Values or Cultural Divorce?*

The European Alliance of EU-Critical Movements (TEAM)
e-mail: jespermorvill@mail.dk
Web site: www.teameurope.info

TEAM is a network connecting fifty-seven EU-critical, or eurosceptic, organizations in twenty-three countries across Europe. TEAM brings together civil organizations and political parties to fight against the emerging EU state and what TEAM views as the erosion of democracy in Europe. There are multiple publications written by their members available at their Web site, including *Europe Deserves Better* and *14-Point Critical Summary of the EU Constitution.*

Virtual Resource Centre for Knowledge About Europe (CVCE)
Chateau de Sanem, Sanem   L-4992
   Luxembourg

352-5959201 • fax: 352-595920555
e-mail: cvce@cvce.lu
Web site: www.cvce.lu

The CVCE utilizes experts in a wide range of disciplines with the aim of promoting and disseminating information about Europe's heritage. The CVCE's main project is the European Navigator (ENA) knowledge base, which contains a wealth of material on European history and the process of European integration. In addition to the information provided on ENA, news and a monthly newsletter are available on its Web site.

Bibliography of Books

Clive Archer   *The European Union: Structure and Process.* 3rd ed. New York: Continuum, 2000.

Ian Bache and   *Politics in the European Union.* 2nd
Stephen George   ed. New York: Oxford University Press, 2006.

Elizabeth   *The European Union: How Does It*
Bomberg and   *Work?* New York: Oxford University
Alexander Stubb   Press, 2003.

Michelle Cini   *European Union Politics.* 2nd ed. New York: Oxford University Press, 2007.

Maria Green   *Developments in the European Union*
Cowles and   *2.* New York: Palgrave Macmillan,
Desmond Dinan,   2004.
eds.

Desmond Dinan   *Europe Recast: A History of European Union.* Boulder, CO: Lynne Rienner, 2004.

Mette   *Debates on European Integration.* New
Eilstrup-   York: Palgrave Macmillan, 2006.
Sangiovanni, ed.

Ralph H. Folsom   *European Union Law in a Nutshell.* St. Paul, MN: West Group, 2005.

Justin Greenwood   *Interest Representation in the European Union.* 2nd ed. New York: Palgrave Macmillan, 2007.

Simon Hix

The Political System of the European Union. 2nd ed. New York: Palgrave Macmillan, 2005.

Jolyon Howorth

Security and Defence Policy in the European Union. New York: Palgrave Macmillan, 2007.

Robert Kagan

Of Paradise and Power: America and Europe in the New World Order. New York: Random House, 2003.

Dick Leonard

Guide to the European Union. 9th ed. New York: Bloomberg, 2005

Christopher Lord

A Democratic Audit of the European Union. New York: Palgrave Macmillan, 2004.

Geir Lundestad

The United States and Western Europe Since 1945: From 'Empire' by Invitation to Transatlantic Drift. New York: Oxford University Press, 2003.

Paul Magnette

What Is the European Union? Nature and Prospects. New York: Palgrave Macmillan, 2005.

Gary Marks and Marco R. Steenbergen, eds.

European Integration and Political Conflict. New York: Oxford University Press, 2004.

Andrew Moravcsik, ed.

Europe Without Illusions. Lanham, MD: University Press of America, 2005.

Neill Nugent, ed.

European Union Enlargement. New York: Palgrave Macmillan, 2004.

John Peterson and Michael Shackleton — *The Institutions of the European Union*. 2nd ed. New York: Oxford University Press, 2006.

Lord Pearson of Rannoch and Stephen Pollard — *Should We Stay or Should We Go? Two Views on Britain and the EU*. London: Civitas, 2005.

T.R. Reid — *The United States of Europe: The New Superpower and the End of American Supremacy*. New York: Penguin, 2004.

Jeremy Rifkin — *The European Dream*. New York: Penguin, 2004.

Andy Smith — *Politics and the European Commission*. London: Routledge, 2004.

David Wood and Birol Yesilada — *The Emerging European Union*. 4th ed. London: Longman, 2006.

Steve Wood and Wolfgang Quaisser — *The New European Union: Confronting the Challenges of Integration*. Boulder, CO: Lynne Rienner, 2007.

Index

A

Accession to EU, 38, 55, 57, 59–62, 67
Accession Treaty, 60
African Union, 90
Agreements. *See* Treaties/agreements
Airbus Industries, 135–137, 141
Algeria, 68
Anti-Turkish sentiment, 74–75
Antiglobalization, 40
Arab-Israeli peace settlement, 111
Ash, Timothy Garton, 26–36
Asmus, Ronald D., 106–113
Association of Southeast Asian Nations (ASEAN), 90, 103

B

Balkan Gap, 80
Bartlett, Bruce, 124–128
Berlin Declaration, 45–46
Bilateral agreements, 62, 66
Blair, Tony (Prime Minister), 85, 143, 156
Blanchard, Olivier J., 119–123
Boeing Company, 136, 142
Bosnia-Herzegovina, 70
Brandt, Willy, 110
Buchanan, Patrick J., 42–46
Bush, George W.
    EU relations, 104, 112
    foreign policy, 143
    NATO, 105
    unilateralism, 103
    U.S./European differences, 108–109

Business globalization, 58
Buy American Act, 142

C

CAP. *See* Common Agricultural Policy
Center for European Reform, 153
Central government site, 115
Centralization, as future action
    constitution, 48
    EU popularity, 49
    euro dollars, 49
    generational divide, 50–51
    immigration/identity, 49–50
    Muslims, 49–50
    nationalism, 50
    needed action, 51–52
    political life, 48
    sovereignty concerns, 48–49
Chicago Council on Foreign Relations, 112
China, 25, 115, 117, 133
CIS-stemming countries, 65
Cold War, 29–30, 100–101, 108–110
Coleman, Vernon, 83–88
Common Agricultural Policy (CAP), 33
Communist dictatorship, 28
Competition policy, 33
Conflict resolution, 29
Constitution disagreement, as sign of democracy
    electoral politics, 40
    future considerations, 41
    lack of democracy, 39–41
    member rejections, 38–39

NAFTA, 38
positive steps, 37
unipolar world, 41
See also Democracy
Copenhagen criteria, 60, 69–70
Council of Ministers, EU, 93
Coutreaux, Paul-Marie, 175
Cultural identity characteristics,
149

D

De Gaulle, Charles, 103–104
Democracy
EU, 93
future vision, 27
Great Britain, 93
lack of, 39–41, 156
languages, 166–171
liberal democratic rule, 27
See also Constitution disagree-
ment, as sign of democracy
Diversity goal, EU, 33–34
Druon, Maurice, 172–176

E

EA. *See* European Agreements
The Economist (journal), 67–71
EEA. *See* European Economic
Area
EEC. *See* European Economic
Community
Elections
Algerian, 68
in EC, 40–41, 93
EU parliamentary, 64, 75, 163
EU vs. U.S., 40
French, 51
German, 71
Great Britain, 48
over Turkish membership, 24

Employment practices, harmful to
EU economy
GDP, 125–126
hourly distribution, 127
IMF, 128
income tax, 124, 128
leisure time, 126
living standards, 125
OECD, 126–128
Employment practices, not harmful to EU economy
vs. China, 133
current model, 131–134
GDP, 131
vs. Germany, 133
growth lags, 132
standard of living, 129
unemployment, 130
wages, 132
WTO, 133
England Our England (Coleman),
87
English Parliament, 87–88
ENP. *See* European Neighborhood
Policy
Environmental benefits, EU, 92
ERASMUS program, 147–148
Ethnic cleansing, 84
Euro dollars
centralization, 49
EU identity, 157
referendum, 156
strength, 41, 116
trashing, 107
withdrawal of, 130
Eurocrats, 38
Euroland's Secret Success Story
(Goldman Sachs), 130
Europe Reborn (James), 32
European Agreements (EA), 62–63
European Commission (EC)
accession criteria, 61

commissioner selection, 40
elections, 40–41, 93
ERASMUS program, 147–148
language necessity, 166–171
as legislative body, 162
Public Opinion Analysis sector, 19–20
success, 92
warfare, 55
European companies, thriving
Airbus Industries, 141
Boeing Company, 142
military, 140, 143–144
Muslim population growth, 144
socialism, 141–142
standard of living, 143
vs. U.S. military power, 143
European companies, unfair advantages for
Airbus Industries, 135–137
Boeing Company, 136
protectionism, 138
subsidies, 136–138
trade war, 138
WTO, 136–137
European Council, 59
European Court of Justice, 176
European Economic Area (EEA), 62
European Economic Community (EEC), 14, 68, 90
European identity, as void
democracy, 156
the euro, 157
failed attempts, 158–159
patriotism, 155, 158
problems, 157–158
statehood trappings, 156
vs. USSR, 158

European identity, compatible with National identity
attitude/values, 154–155
changing attitudes, 151
cultural characteristics, 149
decline, 152
growth, 31
political identity, 153–154
process of, 151–153
transnational members, 150–151
European Monetary Union. See Euro dollars
European Neighborhood Policy (ENP), 65
European Parliament, 40, 93, 170
The European Press, 144
European Union (EU)
accomplishments, 43–44
court of justice, 30
economic integration, 97
ERASMUS program, 147–148
as family likeness, 35–36
freedom of access, 97
global success, 96–98
immigrant workers, 15–16
lack of democracy, 39–41
languages, 146–148
Maastricht Treaty, 15
member states, 19–20, 54–56, 59
nationalism vs. allegiance, 42–46
nationalities, 146–148
origin of, 14–17
politics, 20, 153–154
Schengen Agreement, 15
single market, 98
support of global security, 104–105
unemployment concerns, 19

vs. U.S. military power, 101–102

warfare, 55

European Union (EU), continued expansion

accession, 57, 59–62

bilateral agreements, 62, 66

CIS-stemming countries, 65

Copenhagen criteria, 60

EA, 62–63

EEA, 62

ENP, 65

foreign defense policy, 60–61

globalizing business, 58

PCA, 64

peripheral countries, 62–66

Reform Treaty, 59

Russia, 64–65

SAA, 63

Sahel zone states, 65–66

Single Market, 58, 60–62

Turkey, 63–64

European Union (EU), economy not thriving

GDP, 115

growth rate, 116

member workers, 114

needs, 116

Polish plumber metaphor, 116–118

site of government, 115

trade policy, 117

unemployment rate, 117

vs. U.S., 115

European Union (EU), economy thriving

europessimists, 119–121

gains allocation, 123

GDP, 121–122

growth, 121

PPP, 121

European Union (EU), expansion hurdles

Copenhagen criteria, 69–70

EEC, 68

immigration, 68

joining requirements, 69–70

new member problems, 70–71

opinion poll, 69

stability, 67

European Union (EU) languages, challenges with

demands, 161–162

dominant language, 164–165

multilingualism, 161–162

parliamentary sessions, 161

translation issues, 162–164

vs. UN, 161

European Union (EU) languages, necessity of

democracy, 166, 170–171

legislation, 168

NATO, 171

parliament, 170

European Union Treaty, 59

Europessimists, 119–121

Eurosceptics, 34

F

Foreign defense policy, EU, 60–61

France

constitution by, 44–45, 48

economy, 120

GDP, 122

immigrants, 116

National Front, 50

nationalism, 51

politics, 22

referendums, 23–24, 38

social market economy, 115

tax burden, 128

unemployment levels, 16, 117

French, as EU official language
    arguments for, 173–176
    globalization, 174
Future vision, defined by shared
    goals
    CAP, 33
    communist dictatorship, 28
    competition policy, 33
    conflict resolution, 29
    corruption, 28
    court of justice, 30
    diversity, 33–34
    European identity, 31
    Eurosceptics, 34
    family likeness, 35–36
    free enterprise, 34
    freedom, 27–29
    law, 30–32
    liberal democratic rule, 27
    peace, 29–30
    prosperity, 32–33
    solidarity, 34–35
Future vision, members divided
    challenges, 23–25
    defense, 21
    first fifty years, 22–23
    geopolitics, 24–25
    member countries, 24
    military preparedness, 25
    public opinion gap, 23

G

Gains allocation, EU, 123
GDP. See Gross domestic product
Generational divide, 50–51
Geoghegan, Thomas, 129–134
German Marshall Fund, 112
Germany, 71, 133
Globalization
    vs. antiglobalization, 40
    business, 58

EU vs. Great Britain, 89–90,
    93–94
    French, 174
    official EU language, 174
    postwar world economy, 139
    sovereignty, 48
Great Britain
    democracy, 93
    elections, 48
    globalization, 89–90
    immigration, 44
Great Britain, should leave EU
    disappearing English, 87–88
    ethnic cleansing, 84
    nationalism, 83
    parliament, 87–88
    racism, 87
    Regional Assemblies, 84–85
    support for, 86
    voters ignored, 85–86
Great Britain, should not leave EU
    cooperation needs, 90
    Council of Ministers, 93
    democracy, 93
    EEC, 90
    environmental benefits, 92
    European Parliament, 93
    globalization, 89–90, 93–94
    household income increase, 91
    market benefits, 91
    NAFTA, 90
    REACH, 92
    single market, 91
    success, 92–93
    summary arguments, 93–94
    trade benefits, 91
Greater Middle East, 108–109
Gross domestic product (GDP)
    employment practices, 131
    EU, 121–122
    global security, 100

per person, 125–126
U.S. vs. EU, 115
Gulf War, 100

H

Hannan, Daniel, 155–159
Hussein, Saddam, 109, 111

I

Identity issues. *See* European identity, as void; European identity, compatible with National identity
Immigration/immigrants
  into EU, 45–46
  as expansion hurdle, 68
  French, 116
  Great Britain, 44
  and identity, 49–50
  Muslims, 49–50
  workers, 15–16
Income tax, EU economy, 124, 128
International idealism, 101
International Monetary Fund (IMF), 128
Investor's Business Daily (newspaper), 135–139
Iraq, invasion of, 100
Islamic extremism, 144

J

James, Harold, 32
James, Kyle, 149–154

K

Kaczynski, Lech, 50
Kagan, Robert, 99–105
Kopstein, Jeffrey, 21–25
Kupchan, Charles, 47–52

L

Labor balance, 80
Laming, Richard, 89–94
Law goals, 30–32
Leisure time, EU vs. U.S., 126
Lesson of Munich, 101
Liberal democratic rule, 27

M

Maastricht Treaty, 15
Market benefits, EU, 91
McKay, Floyd J., 140–144
Member countries
  map, 24
  new succession, 38, 67
  politics divided, 24–25
  transnational nature of, 150–151
  workers, 114
Merkel, Angela (Chancellor), 45, 51
Military preparedness, EU, 25, 112, 140, 143–144
Military strategy, U.S., 100, 102–104, 143
Multilingualism, 161–162
Muslims
  accession, 75, 79, 81
  in Bosnia, 70
  centralization, 49–50
  immigrants, 48–50
  in non-Arab countries, 82
  population growth, 144

N

National Front, France, 50
Nationalism vs. EU allegiance
  accomplishments, 43–44
  Berlin Declaration, 45–46
  centralization, 50

future considerations, 42
Great Britain, 83
immigrants, 45–46
peace, 75–76
popularity, 44–45
Turkey, 72
UK immigration, 44
Non-Arab Muslim countries, 82
North American Free Trade Agreement (NAFTA), 38, 90
North Atlantic Treaty Organization (NATO), 28–29, 79, 104–105, 171

O

Ode to Joy (EU anthem), 38, 156, 158
Organization for Economic Cooperation and Development (OECD), 126–128
Ostpolitik (Brandt), 110
Owens, James, 160–165

P

Pamuk, Orhan, 72–76
Partnership and cooperation agreements (PCA), 64
Patriotism, European identity, 155, 158
Patton, Chris, 156–157
Peace goals, EU, 29–30
Petrucci, Pietro, 176
Polish plumber metaphor, 116–118
Politics
electoral, 40
EU centralization, 48
EU concerns, 20
EU identity, 153–154
of France, 22
geopolitics, 24–25

member countries divided, 24–25
Pollack, Kenneth M., 106–113
Prodi, Romano (Prime Minister), 51
Prosperity goals, EU, 32–33
Public Opinion Analysis sector, EC, 19–20
Purchasing power parity (PPP), 121

R

Racism, 87
Rahn, Richard W., 114–118
Reagan, Ronald, 110
Reform Treaty, 59
Regional Assemblies, Great Britain, 84–85
Registration, Evaluation and Authorization of Chemicals (REACH), 92
Religious differences, 76, 79
Rumsfeld, Donald, 141
Russia, 64–65, 70, 81
Ryder Cup, 159

S

SAA. *See* Stabilisation and association agreements
Sahel zone states, 65–66
Schengen Agreement, 15
September 11, 2001, global security, 100–101, 107
Single market
benefits, 91
commissioner, 70
continued expansion, 58, 60–62, 147
goal success, 92, 97–98
Great Britain, 91

official language, 167
size, 122
Social market economy, 115
Socialism, 141–142
Solidarity, 34–35
Sovereignty concerns, 48–49
Soviet Union (USSR), 158
Spencer, Tom, 77–82
Stabilisation and association agreements (SAA), 63
Standard of living, 129, 143
Statehood trappings, 156
Supranatural governance, 102

T

Terrorism
civil liberties, 32
EU concerns, 19, 112
September 11, 2001, 100–101, 107
Trade
EU benefits, 91
policies, 117
surplus, 138–139
war, EU vs. U.S., 138
Translator's Workbench, 164
Treaties/agreements
Accession, 60
bilateral, 62, 66
EA, 62–63
European Union, 59
Reform, 59
Rome, 22, 28
SAA, 63
Schengen, 15
Treaty Establishing the European Community (TEC), 14
The Truth They Won't Tell You About the EU (Coleman), 87
Turkey, 24, 63–64

Turkey, EU accession should be allowed
anti-Turkish sentiment, 74–75
benefits, 74
European sentiment, 74–75
Muslims, 75
nationalism, 72
novel as way of understanding, 73–74
peace vs. nationalism, 75–76
religious differences, 76, 79
Turkey, EU accession should not be allowed
arguments, 78–79
Balkan Gap, 80
geography, 78–79
historical perspective, 81–82
integration, 77
labor balance, 80
Muslims, 79, 81
NATO, 79
priorities, 79–81
treaty definitions, 78

U

Unemployment
concerns, 19
French, 16, 117
practices, 130
rates, 117
Unilateralism, 102–103
Unipolar world, 41
United Nations (UN)
cooperation needs, 90
military preparedness, 25, 112
official language, 161, 171, 176
U.S. contribution, 144
U.S. global security, EU help needed
Bush administration, 108–109
commonality, 108–110
cooperation, 111–113
disputes/differences, 107–108

joint strategy, 106, 110–111
September 11, 2001, 107
terrorist attack, 112
transatlantic cooperation, 108
U.S. global security, maintenance of
  ASEAN, 103
  Bush administration, 104
  vs. European, 101–102
  European support, 99, 104–105
  GDP, 100
  international idealism, 101
  lesson of Munich, 101

military power/strategy, 100, 102–104
September 11, 2001, 100–101
supranatural governance, 102
unilateralism, 102–103
USSR. *See* Soviet Union

W

Wages, 132
World Trade Organization (WTO), 133, 136–137

Y

Younge, Gary, 37–41

CPSIA information can be obtained
at www.ICGtesting.com
Printed in the USA
LVHW050424280122
709355LV00016B/1881